Robert & Eleanor Bizinsky
1952 – 1982

Britain's

W. M?COWELL

THE OFFICIAL PICTORIAL HISTORY

THE QUEEN MARY

Text by Robert O. Maguglin
Historical Consultant: Bill M. Winberg

ce — R.M.S. "QUEEN MARY"

WRATHER PORT PROPERTIES, LTD., LONG BEACH, CALIFORNIA

Engine telegraph from the ship's bridge is used to send maneuvering commands to the engine room.

A C K N O W L E D G E M E N T S

Thank you to the following who made special contributions to this publication: Richard Radstone; Alex Marshall Linda Davis (editing); Nicky Leach (coordination):

A special thanks to Bill Winberg of Wrather Port Properties for his research and consultation.

Many of the staff of Wrather Port Properties and The Queen Mary assisted throughout and showed great patience and consideration.

And most of all, to Jack and Bonita Granville Wrather, for their vision in making the Queen Mary available to future generations and preserving this unique legacy for all.

Produced for Wrather Port Properties by Sequoia Communications, Inc.
Design: Mary Schlesinger, Schlesinger Design
Type: Friedrich Typography
Printed in Japan
Library of Congress no. 85-050967
ISBN: 0-86679-023-3

Cunard White Star publicity poster showing the Queen Mary, Aquitania, *and* Berengaria.

P H O T O G R A P H Y

C O N T E N T S

*Early artist's rendering of the Queen Mary showing passengers
lounging and strolling on the proposed liner's spacious Sun Deck.*

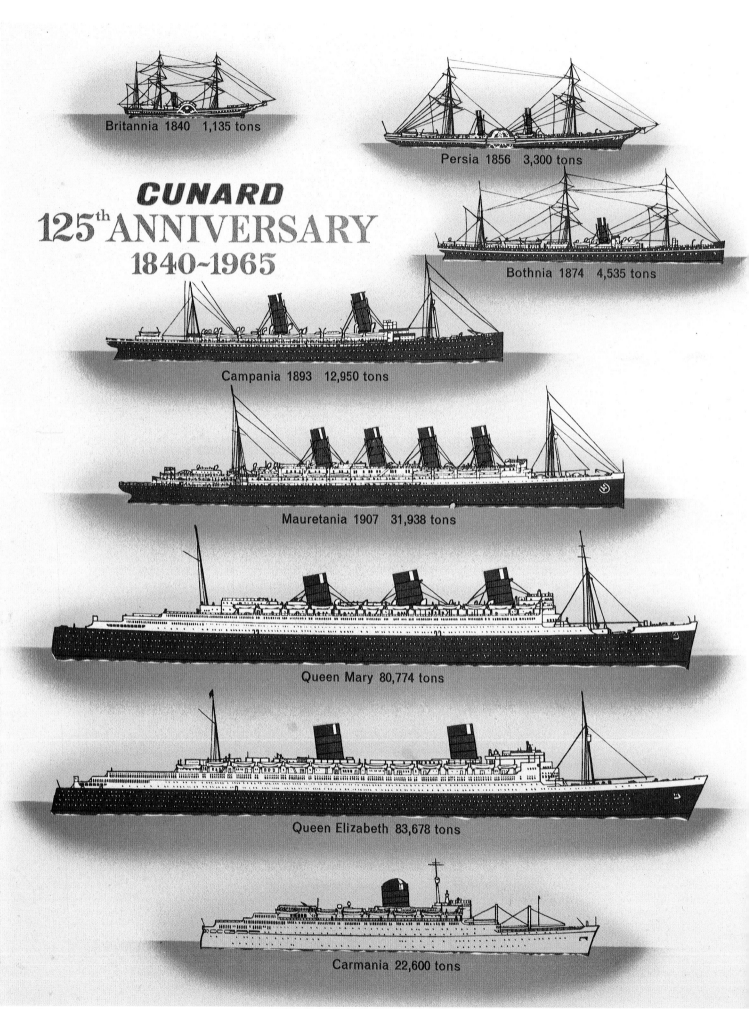

Britannia 1840 1,135 tons

Persia 1856 3,300 tons

Bothnia 1874 4,535 tons

CUNARD
125ᵗʰ ANNIVERSARY
1840~1965

Campania 1893 12,950 tons

Mauretania 1907 31,938 tons

Queen Mary 80,774 tons

Queen Elizabeth 83,678 tons

Carmania 22,600 tons

Special Cunard 125th Anniversary menu cover celebrates a progression of the company's most famous ships.

BIRTH OF THE
SUPERLINERS

Workmen are dwarfed by one of the ship's massive 35-ton manganese-bronze propellers. Each blade is seven feet high, yet the propellers are so perfectly balanced, they can be turned by hand.

Chapter I

The Queen Mary, perhaps the most illustrious ship in history, began as a single line on a piece of paper in 1926 as the planning committee of the Cunard Steamship Company contemplated the modernization of its passenger ship fleet.

Cunard was in a precarious position. For decades, the company was in the forefront of the transatlantic steamship trade. But after World War I, it began falling behind.

Cunard's prized luxury liner, the Lusitania, was sunk at the beginning of the war and, during the course of the conflict, many other Cunard vessels followed her to the bottom. At the war's end, German, French, Italian, and American shipyards and maritime companies began to challenge Britain's pre-eminent position on the high seas.

Then, following firmly in the footsteps of the shipping line's legendary founder, Samuel Cunard, the planning committee prepared to take a bold step into the future — a step upon which the company's financial future and that of its thousands of employees depended.

Confering with the Cunard staff of designers and marine architects, the company's top executives examined the requirements to modernize its fleet. They envisioned weekly sailings from New York and Southampton involving two ships instead of the three then required, a reduction that would provide great economic relief through reduced operating, personnel, and fuel costs. To maintain the weekly schedule, however, the two transatlantic liners had to be faster than any existing ship. The minimum cruising speed necessary to keep the schedule was 28½ knots (32.8 mph/52.8 kmh); and to achieve this, the vessel had to be larger than any ship then in service in order to house the massive machinery needed to increase its speed.

Shipyard workmen put finishing touches on one of the Queen's *steel masts.*

Thirty-five-ton propeller is a real attention-getter as it leaves the Manganese Bronze & Brass Co., Ltd. factory in Millwall, London, for its journey to Southampton to be fitted on the Queen Mary. *The ship's four props were the world's largest.*

Since the first ships sailed the Atlantic Ocean, speed, size, and mechanical complexity of the vessels continually increased. The earliest known people to cross the mighty Atlantic were the Vikings, who sailed to the New World in frail longboats. The Scandinavians were followed by adventurous Europeans in small squat ships exploring the North and South American coasts.

As colonies sprouted in North America, Europe coveted the wealth of the new land, and their need for reliable transportation to cross the Atlantic became a principal concern. Over time, sea-going vessels evolved into efficient sailing packets (mail ships which sailed on regular schedules dictated by the weather and tides).

The epitome of sailing was reached with the advent of clipper ships. Slim, sturdy, well-built, these vessels were able to withstand all but the severest of the ocean's furies. The clippers were swift sailing ships, but with the vagaries of time and tide, a crossing from England to New York could take thirty days or more. And as strong as the clippers were, many ships still succumbed to the violence of the North Atlantic weather. Passengers sailed out of necessity, not for pleasure, and with the knowledge that they might not survive the crossing. In addition, the rigors of shipboard life were grim. Passengers' quarters were cramped and overcrowded. Food on the long voyage was substandard and, during storms or even heavy seas, no cooking was possible.

But the invention of the steam engine promised a bright future for the transatlantic trade. Ships crossed the Atlantic in the early 1800s using a combination of steam and sails. Then, in April 1838, the Sirius steamed from Cork, Ireland, to New York in nineteen days without the aid of its auxiliary sails.

The Queen's *huge cast-steel stern frame takes shape at the Darlington Forge. Weighing 190 tons, it was the largest in the world.*

Job number 534's size makes workmen appear tiny in comparison. In the foreground, the Second Class Swimming Pool is taking shape; in the upper portion of the photo, two massive main strongbeams mark space for the engine rooms.

Illustration depicts Samuel Cunard's first steamship, the Britannia, *making her way through a narrow channel cut into the ice on Bonston Harbor in February 1844. Boston merchants had the 100-foot-wide, seven-mile-long channel cut to allow the Cunarder to use the harbor. The vessel is shown departing for Liverpool.*

Atlantic crossings by steam vessels after the Sirus' successful voyage were numerous yet sporadic. A sailing ship might have to wait weeks for favorable weather or tides before sailing, making it impossible to schedule departures and arrivals.

Samuel Cunard, in his effort to standardize the occasional adventurous crossings of the Atlantic, saw the steamships as the means of achieving a great purpose. He realized that a reliable steamship service could be very profitable, especially in the transportation of mail between the continents.

In 1838, the British government invited bids from commercial companies to carry mail on the Atlantic, and Cunard formed the British and North American Royal Mail Steam Packet Company, later renamed the Cunard Steamship Company. He ordered his first ship, the Britannia, from a Scottish shipbuilding firm. She had paddle wheels amidships on either side of her hull, was 207 feet long, weighed 1,154 tons, and could carry 225 tons of cargo and 115 passengers at a cruising speed of 9 knots (10.4 mph/16.7 kmh).

The Britannia set sail on her maiden voyage from Liverpool to Boston via Halifax on July 4, 1840. She arrived in Halifax in 12 days and 10 hours with an average speed of 8 knots (9.2 mph/14.8 kmh) for the 3,000-mile crossing. The Britannia was soon followed by her sisterships, the new Cunarders Acadia, Caledonia, and Columbia. From this small beginning, Samuel Cunard built the company that eventually reaped the lion's share of the transatlantic passenger trade.

It was not long before marine designers planned larger vessels with greater speed, in an attempt to use three ships instead of four to maintain weekly crossings of the Atlantic. Technological advancement concerning the company's transatlantic vessels was rapid in the Cunard Steamship Company. The wooden hull gave way to iron in 1852 with the Andes, and the paddle wheel was superseded by the screw propeller in 1862 with the

One of the Queen's 16 turbine rotors. Each of the ship's 257,000 turbine blades was individually set by hand to ensure perfect alignment.

China. Passenger accommodations became more comfortable and, in the 1870s, the first ships with private bathrooms and Promenade Decks, upon which passengers could stroll and relax, were launched. Steel hulls replaced iron in 1881 with the Servia, the first Cunarder to be illuminated with electric lights. Twin propellers debuted on the liners Campania and Lucania. Steam turbine machinery replaced reciprocating engines in 1905 with the Carmania. Each new generation of steamship was larger, faster, and more comfortable than the last.

The financial reward of owning the swiftest ship could not be ignored. Passengers wanted to travel on the fleetest ships, and the vessel holding the record for the fastest crossing was always in great demand.

After World War I, with the Mauretania, Aquitania, and Berengaria (ex-Imperator), Cunard implemented a three-ship service providing weekly sailings between New York and England, made possible by the 22- to 25-knot service speeds (25.3 to 28.8 mph/40.7 to 46.3 kmh) of these three ships. When coal gave way to oil-fired boilers in 1920, marine technology reached a stage where the ultimate goal of a two-ship service became feasible. And in 1926, the planning committee of the Cunard Steamship Company was ready to make the goal a reality.

Workmen use a giant-sized chain in preparation for lifting huge steel frame weighing 190 tons.

Sparks fly at Beardmore Parkhead Forge in Glasgow as a workman prepares castings for the new Cunarder.

Although the ship eventually became one of the fastest and largest vessels ever built, it was initially designed as the "slowest and smallest" ship capable of maintaining an average cruising speed of 28½ knots, and of adequate size to carry enough cargo and passengers to pay its operational costs. The final blueprints called for a total length of 1,019½ feet and a gross tonnage of 81,237, nearly twice that of the ill-fated Titanic.

It was soon apparent that the liner's size created problems. Nothing so large had ever been built, and the design taxed the skill and craftsmanship of both the designers and the builders. An adequate drydock did not exist, nor was a launching facility available. More importantly, existing docking facilities on both sides of the Atlantic were not capable of handling a ship of that size.

But one by one the problems were solved. The Southern Railways Company agreed to construct a huge stationary graving dock in Southampton, and New York and Southampton port authorities consented to build facilities to accommodate the giant liner.

With these major obstructions removed, serious planning began on the new ship. For two years, naval architects and planners worked out the details of construction. Thousands of tank tests were conducted to determine the vessel's hull shape and propeller design. Wind tunnel tests were performed to ensure that the ship's funnels properly carried smoke and fumes away from the passenger decks. Comparisons were made, and the most efficient propulsion system for the giant liner was carefully chosen.

Cunard's Mauretania, which held the transatlantic speed record with the Lusitania for a combined twenty-two years, was a steam turbine vessel with coal-fired boilers that were later replaced by oil-fired boilers. But advances in both turbo-electric and diesel engines interested the Cunard designers. They finally decided that steam turbine engines using a single reduction gear would provide the best engine performance. The single reduction gear allowed the turbines to spin at high speeds while the propellers revolved at slow speeds, at which the two pieces of machinery were most efficient.

Job number 534 serves as a mute symbol of modern-day technology, contrasting sharply with the rural farmer across the Clyde River, cutting his crop with a Clydesdale-horse-drawn reaper.

Finally, in December 1930, the first rivet was ceremoniously placed in the longest keel ever laid in a British shipyard. John Brown & Company, Clydebank, Scotland, was chosen by Cunard to build Job Number 534, the only designation the ship carried until her christening and launch.

The ship's hull soon rose high over the shipyard, and sightseers on the River Clyde marveled at the enormous steel behemoth taking shape before their eyes.

But one year after construction began, disaster struck. The Great Depression hit England hard, and Cunard found itself in financial difficulty. Drastic cost-cutting measures were adopted to save the company from bankruptcy, but they were not enough. All work on Job Number 534 came to an abrupt halt on December 10, 1931; Cunard did not have the funds to finish the great liner.

The winter was bleak for the Clydebank workmen and their families. One observer wrote, ". . . the great vessel — no longer reverberating to the rhythm of the hammers — lay silent, a symbol of the cold hand of economic stress which lay on the hearts of the people." Thousands of jobs were lost all over Great Britain, when shops and factories fabricating or preparing to fabricate parts, fixtures, and accessories for the new ship were forced to cancel production and lay off employees.

For more than two years, the ship's unfinished hull towered above the quiet shipyard, a stark symbol of the grim hardship that held the people of Great Britain in its grip. During these years, other governments stepped in to aid their shipbuilding and maritime industries. France's government subsidized the continuing construction of the liner Normandie, while in Great Britain, the issue of government assistance for Job Number 534 was cautiously debated in Parliament. But not until 1934 was a satisfactory agreement reached.

The British government agreed to finance Job Number 534 and her sistership, but required that Cunard merge with England's other great transatlantic shipping line, White Star. Early in 1934, the two companies became the Cunard White Star Line and, on April 3, 1934, work resumed on Job Number 534. It was a joyous day for all of Great Britain, but especially for the Clydebank workers and their long-suffering families. The men marched lightheartedly back into the shipyard, led by bagpipers and cheered by hundreds of the town's residents.

When work resumed on job number 534 in April 1934, after a lapse of nearly three years due to the Great Depression, it was a joyous occasion for all Clydeside residents, most of whom depended upon the shipyard for their livelihood. The liner's hull towers over the village streets as the "Clydesiders" march proudly back to work.

Number "534"

Dockworkers handle the Queen's heavy hawsers as the ship is maneuvered into Southampton's King George drydock.

For ages you were rock, far below light,
Crushed' without shape, earth's unregarded bone.
Then Man in all the marvel of his might
Quarried you out and burned you from the stone.

Then, being pured to essence, you were nought
But weight and hardness, body without nerve;
Then Man in all the marvel of his thought,
Smithied you into form of leap and curve;

And took you, so, and bent you to his vast,
Intense great world of passionate design,
Curve after changing curving, braced and masst
To stand all tumult that can tumble brine,

And left you, this, a rampart of a ship,
Long as a street and lofty as a tower,
Ready to glide in thunder from the slip
And shear the sea with majesty of power.

I long to see you leaping to the urge
Of the great engines, rolling as you go,
Parting the seas in sunder in a surge,
Shredding a trackway like a mile of snow

With all the wester streaming from your hull
And all gear twanging shrilly as you race,
And effortless above your stern a gull
Leaning upon the blast and keeping place.

May shipwreck and collision, fog and fire,
Rock, shoal and other evils of the sea,
Be kept from you; and may the heart's desire
Of those who speed your launching come to be.

John Masefield

To commemorate the launch of Great Britain's greatest liner, British Poet Laureate John Masefield wrote this special poem, appropriately entitled Number 534.

One of the vessel's 40,000 horsepower steam turbine engines is tested in John Brown's engineering shop before being reassembled in the Queen Mary's hull.

The Secret of a Name

When the time came to launch the partially-completed hull and christen it with a name, all of Great Britain held its collective breath. The company had kept the name for the new ship a closely guarded secret. Many thought Cunard would continue its tradition of choosing names ending in "-ia" (as in Lusitania and Mauretania), while others believed the name would end in "-ic" (as did White Star's Titanic and Olympic, for example). Some astute observers predicted that, to accommodate the consolidation of the two shipping lines, the new ship's name would be the first of an entirely new style. Interest in the naming of Job Number 534 became intense. Although the subject of widespread newspaper and radio speculation, the Cunarder's name remained secret until the official christening.

September 26, 1934, dawned with cold winds and heavily overcast skies. Rain fell intermittently throughout the day. At the John Brown & Company shipyard, thousands of spectators huddled together, shivering in the biting cold. Every inch of available space was occupied by an estimated 200,000 curious Britons, anxious to witness the launch of the greatest vessel ever built. On the River Clyde, boats were jammed with additional sightseers. For every Briton, the new Cunarder was special. It was their ship, the pride of British art and craftsmanship and a symbol of the indomitable spirit of a nation recovering from economic ruin — the ship they hoped would reclaim Great Britain's place of honor on the North Atlantic.

Soon, the secret of the new liner's name would be revealed. On hand to perform this historic christening was Her Majesty Queen Mary. For the first time in Great Britain's history, a reigning queen was to christen a merchant vessel, an unprecedented occasion. But no one foresaw the actual significance of Her Majesty's participation.

During the pre-launch ceremonies, King George V spoke to the crowd. His speech was short but effective, closing with the words, "Today, we can send her forth no longer a number on the books, but a ship with a name . . . alive with beauty, energy, and strength . . . the stateliest ship now in being . . ."

Then, Her Majesty Queen Mary stepped forward to the microphone. A hush of expectancy fell over the crowd. With nervous dignity, the Queen gently snipped the satin cord holding a bottle of Australian white wine, sending it crashing against the bow plates of Job Number 534. As the bottle shattered, she pressed a small button to fire the launch triggers, and her voice rang out, "I am happy to name this ship the Queen Mary. I wish success to her and to all who sail in her."

The crowd exploded with a roar of approval. No finer name could have been chosen for Great Britain's new *Monarch of the Seas* than that of their beloved Queen Mary — the first time in history that a merchant vessel bore the name of a reigning queen.

With the words, ". . . I am happy to name this ship the Queen Mary. *I wish success to her and to all who sail in her,* "Her Majesty pressed a button which sent the massive hull sliding down the ways and into the waters of the River Clyde.*

Ornate ceremonial scissors used to snip the ribbon which sent a bottle of Australian white wine crashing against the bow plates of the newest and largest Cunard liner during the christening ceremony. These same scissors were later used at the launching ceremonies of the Queen Elizabeth *and* QE2.

THIS CASKET WAS WROUGHT FOR HER MAJESTY, QUEEN MARY, BY COMMAND OF JOHN BROWN & COMPANY TO MARK THE OCCASION OF

THE LARGEST VESSEL THAT EVER TOOK THE WATER

LEIF ERICSSON Circa 900 A.D

The MAYFLOWER 1620

The SANTA MARIA 1492

HER MAJESTY'S GRACIOUS ACT in LAUNCHING at their CLYDEBANK SHIPYARD on SEPTEMBER 26TH 1934 The CUNARD WHITE STAR EXPRESS LINER No 534

Lid of special commemorative casket presented to Her Majesty Queen Mary by the John Brown Shipyard. The lovely chest is hand-wrought and chiseled steel, mounted in gold- and silverplate.

King George V and Queen Mary greet thousands of spectators who thronged into the John Brown Shipyard to watch the new liner's launch.

19

A medallion found on the cover of a booklet commemorating the launch of the ship, printed after the ceremonies.

Ready for launch, the awe-inspiring hull of job number 534 looms over the shipyard. Cribbing blocks have been placed beneath the hull, and tons of tallow grease the slipways. Drag chains to slow the ship's momentum into the water dangle from the hull.

One humorous, but probably fanciful, story surrounding the naming of the RMS Queen Mary has circulated for some time. As the story goes, the Cunard Board of Directors decided to name their newest and greatest ship after the late Queen Victoria, a lady of regal and imperial bearing, herself a symbol of the might and sovereignty of Great Britain. In order to name a merchant vessel after a member of the royal family, the King's permission was needed. Meeting with King George V, the Chairman of Cunard asked, "Your Majesty, we would like your permission to name Job Number 534 after Great Britain's most illustrious queen." King George smiled and replied, "Wonderful! I'm sure my wife will be very pleased." And so the new vessel was named the Royal Mail Ship Queen Mary.

A wonderful story, but most certainly a fantasy. In any event, Queen Mary was one of England's most-loved queens. When she christened Job Number 534 with her own name, it was with national approval and acclaim, and the RMS Queen Mary carried her royal name to the far corners of the earth and into the hearts of millions.

The launch button the Queen had pressed fired small electrically released triggers holding the massive hull in place on the launch ways. For twenty-four seconds, nothing seemed to happen; then, with a low groan that rose quickly in intensity, the mammoth hull slid toward the water of the River Clyde. As the vessel moved down the ways, 2,300 tons of drag chains unraveled to slow the ship's momentum. When the hull hit the water, it sent a two-foot wave across the Clyde to lap over the feet of spectators crowding the riverbank. The entire launch took just 112 seconds, one second longer than engineers predicted.

The ship was afloat, dwarfing the tugboats rushing in to shepherd the enormous hull to dockside, where it was tied up. With the launch successfully accomplished, work resumed to finish the ship. Her huge boilers and engines were installed, and the superstructure was completed.

This new ship was ultimately known as "the inevitable ship." Hundreds of years of progress and experience in the art and craft of shipbuilding converged with the Queen Mary. When the ship sailed on her maiden voyage in 1936, twenty months after her launch, she was the ultimate passenger vessel. In later years, more modern ships were built — two ships were larger and one was faster — but the Queen Mary represented the high-water mark in transatlantic travel.

Afloat! With a mighty groan, the massive hull, now officially named the Queen Mary, *slides gracefully into the waters of the River Clyde. More than 2,000 tons of drag chains (attached to the ship's hull) slow, then stop, the ship's momentum. A two-foot wave splashes spectators on the opposite side of the river.*

The Queen Mary's *first captain, Cunard Commodore Sir Edgar Britten, inspects one of the ship's 16-ton anchors.*

Opposite Page:
Workmen install two of the ship's three whistles.
Each whistle weighs one ton and is seven feet long.
Tuned to low "A," the whistles can be heard for ten
miles at sea.

After launching, work continues on the ship's upper
superstructure. Arched supports for lifeboat davits
form a canopy down the length of the Sun Deck.

Shipyard workmen leave the Queen
Mary *at the end of a workday.*

Opposite Page:
Painters put finishing touches on the Queen's paint job.
Each letter in the ship's name is 2½ feet high; the entire
name stretches for more than 55 feet.

23

Girls of the Queen Mary School in Lytham present the Queen Mary's captain, Sir Edgar Britten, with a special blue ensign. The flag, sewn by the girls for the ship, was flown on the maiden voyage.

Noted British artist Edward Wadsworth at work on his painting, Dressed Overall at the Quay, *in the First Class Smoking Lounge.*

A fantasyland for children. Workmen install play equipment and artwork in the First Class Children's Playroom, which even had a full-size slide (at right). Princess Elizabeth (later Queen Elizabeth II) was the first to zoom down the slide.

The Observation Bar still functions today. Inserts show the colorful characters featured in the painting The Royal Jubilee Week, 1935 *by A. R. Thompson, depicting the celebration of King George V's 25th year as king.*

Workers install bar equipment (lower photo) in the Observation Bar, destined to become one of the most popular public rooms on the Queen Mary. Marvelously decorated in a pleasing array of Art Deco color schemes and artwork, the "OB" offered a breathtaking view of the sea over the ship's bow.

This cast likeness of Her Majesty Queen Mary hangs in a place of honor over the main staircase on Promenade Deck.

osite Page:

lling lighting pylons in First Class
ng Room. The beautiful pillars of light
decorated with intricate panels of
ed glass. One of these lovely lightning
ns is now on display in Piccadilly Circus,
ship's main shopping square on
nenade Deck.

of the North Atlantic from the
Class Dining Room. Passengers
d follow the ship's course as a crystal
moved across the map.

Downriver to the Sea

On March 24, 1936, the Queen Mary was ready to leave the shipyard. Tugboats gently nudged the giant liner into the narrow channel of the River Clyde, parts of which were widened to allow the ship's passage. Once in mid-channel, the *Queen's* massive propellers began to move the ship downstream. Vigilant tugboats stayed alongside to maneuver the ship around the river's tight turns. Still, the Queen Mary ran aground twice. Fortunately, the ship was not damaged, and the flotilla of tugboats pulled her free. After completing her sea trials, the *Queen* steamed to Southampton to begin final preparation for her maiden voyage scheduled May 27, 1936 — just one day after the 69th birthday of Her Majesty Queen Mary.

The Queen Mary's *First Class Dining Room, now called the Grand Salon, is the largest room ever built on a ship. It is three decks high, 143 feet long, and 118 feet wide (the entire width of the liner). The room is so large that it can accommodate the entire length of Cunard's first ship, the* Britannia, *plus Columbus'* Nina, Pinta, *and* Santa Maria.

As the Queen Mary *was maneuvered down the Clyde River enroute from the shipyard to open sea, a gust of wind caught the liner. Before the captain or crew could react, the huge ship turned broadside in the river. Her stern went aground and tugboats rushed in, quickly pulling the* Queen *to safety.*

An early rendering shows the magnificent elegance and incredible size of the new liner's main dining salon. All 800 of the ship's first class passengers could be served at one sitting.

QUEEN MARY:

THE PRIDE
OF GREAT BRITAIN

The Queen Mary kicks up wake during maneuvering trials off the Isle of Aran in April 1936. In this photo, the Queen has a "bone in her teeth," a nautical expression used to describe the white water frothing high on her bow, a clear indicaton of a vessel steaming at high speed.

chapter II

CUNARD HOUSE FLAG

On May 25, 1936, King Edward VIII and his royal party arrived at the Ocean Dock in Southampton to visit the Queen Mary. With him were the Duke and Duchess of York (later King George VI and Queen Elizabeth); their daughter Princess Elizabeth (later Queen Elizabeth II); the Duke and Duchess of Kent; the Duchess of Gloucester; and the most honored member of the royal party, Queen Mary, who was seeing the ship for the first time since christening her.

Two days later, the massive seven-foot whistles of the Queen Mary shattered the air with mighty blasts, signaling the beginning of the ship's first passenger voyage. On board were 1,742 passengers — 708 first class, 631 tourist class, and 403 third class — and a crew of 1,186 men and women.

A remarkable cutaway drawing shows the amazing diversity and conplexity of the Queen Mary's *passenger and engine compartments.*

The Cunard Line House Flag with its proud gold lion, flown throughout the Queen Mary's peacetime career.

A close-up of some of the intricate glasswork from the Verandah Grill.

Passengers enjoy an evening of music and conversation in the ship's First Class Ballroom.

A re-creation of the Verandah Grill, the Queen Mary's most exclusive dining room and night spot. Usually, tables had to be reserved months in advance of sailing. While all meals were included in the price of passage, dining in the Verandah Grill was an extra charge.

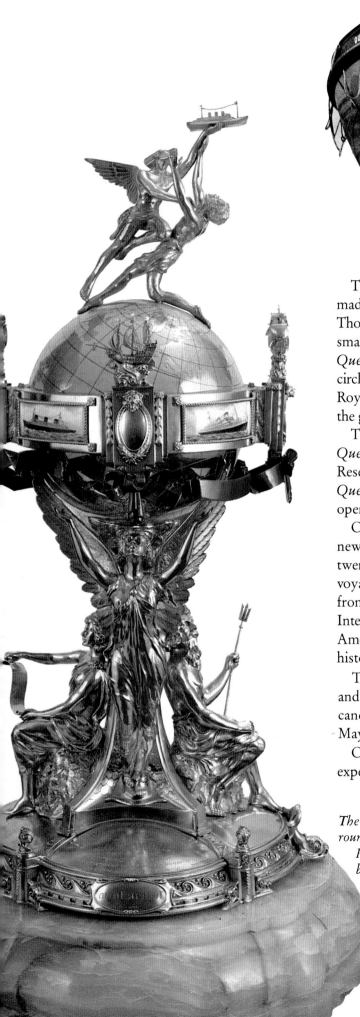

The people of Great Britain had waited ten years for this day, and they made the most of it. Nothing was too good for their country's prize liner. Thousands of cheering spectators lined the docks, while hundreds of small boats, from paddle steamers to row boats, bobbed along in the *Queen's* wake as she slowly made her way toward the open sea. Overhead, circling airplanes carried reporters and photographers. On the dock, the Royal Marine Corps band played "Rule Britannia" as six tugboats assisted the giant ship on her way.

The blue ensign was hoisted up the mainmast, signifying that the *Queen's* Captain, Commodore Sir Edgar Britten, was a Royal Naval Reserve Officer. Signaling the tugboats with a blast of her whistles, the *Queen* steamed up the Solent River and moved majestically toward the open sea.

On board for the maiden voyage were more than 100 reporters and newspapermen. The British Broadcasting Corporation had installed twenty-three remote microphones throughout the ship, and during the voyage, twenty broadcasters from five countries conducted live broadcasts from locations such as the engine rooms, bridge, and Main Lounge. Interest in the Queen Mary extended across the Atlantic as well — two American companies had also sent teams of radio newsmen to record the historic maiden voyage.

The ship's crew loaded 6,124 sacks of mail bound for the United States and Canada. All over the world, stamp collectors eyed the coveted cancellation "Posted at sea, via RMS Queen Mary Maiden Voyage, May 27, 1936."

On B Deck, the *Queen's* three telephone operators prepared for the expected barrage of phone calls as soon as the ship cleared port. The

The Hales Trophy, which was presented to the ship with the fastest North Atlantic round-trip crossing time. Originated by Harold K. Hales, a member of British Parliament, the trophy was administered by an international committee headed by the Duke of Sutherland. Although the Queen Mary *held the speed record for 14 years, Cunard refused to accept the Hales Trophy. It was Cunard's policy not resort to speed for speed's sake. They insisted that the* Queen's *speed runs were to provide data for future ship designs.*

Queen Mary had 600 telephone receivers, one in every first-class cabin and dozens in other locations available to all passengers. The first ship to have a sophisticated ship-to-shore radio-telephone system, the *Queen* not only allowed passengers to ring each other cabin-to-cabin, but also anywhere in the world they called home, even while in mid-Atlantic.

Upon leaving Southampton, the Queen Mary sailed across the channel to Cherbourg, France, to embark an additional 107 passengers and mail. In Cherbourg, the *Queen*'s first stowaway, a Canadian woman journalist, who decried the exclusion of women reporters on the ship's maiden voyage and decided to stow away as a bid for publicity, quietly disembarked before the ship sailed for New York. Later, her adventure was reported in newspapers around the world.

During the crossing, the *Queen*'s second stowaway was discovered: 41-year-old Frank Gardner, an unemployed laborer from Cardiff. He walked aboard posing as a greaser and hid in the number one cargo hold. Gardner was put to work during the voyage helping the kitchen staff, but once the *Queen* reached New York, he was promptly arrested and shipped back to England.

The Blue Riband

Captain Sir Edgar Britten (shaking hands) and Chief Engineer L. Roberts are greeted by Southampton dignitaries after the Queen Mary's recordbreaking run in August 1936. The liner crossed the North Atlantic in under four days, the first ship ever to do so.

Both sides of the Atlantic waited breathlessly to see if the Queen Mary would break the transatlantic speed record held by France's Normandie. Cunard traditionally denied the company was interested in speed records — eventually insisting that the *Queen*'s record-breaking crossing was mainly a trial run for her soon-to-be-built sistership — but they knew a ship's speed had a direct effect on its profits since passengers flocked to the fleetest liner. So intense was the competition to be fastest, an unofficial but highly coveted prize was created: the Blue Riband, symbolized by the exquisitely crafted solid-silver trophy donated in 1935 by British Member of Parliament Harold Hales. The ship capturing the prize garnered tremendous prestige.

Queen Mary's captain, Sir Edgar Britten, on the bridge during the ship's maiden voyage.

Cunard held the distinction of owning the fastest ships from 1907 to 1929. During those twenty-two years, the Mauretania and Lusitania maintained the crossing records (the Mauretania for nineteen years, the Lusitania for two years). But the German liner Bremen captured the record from the aging Mauretania in 1929, passing it to her sistership, the Europa, in 1930. The Italian liner Rex set the record in 1933 and held it until 1935, when the Normandie captured it on her maiden voyage.

The much-asked question in 1936 was, "Would the Queen Mary recapture the Blue Riband for Great Britain, and could she do it on her maiden voyage?" Unfortunately, the *Queen* was slowed by fog, and did not make a record crossing. As far back as 1840, Samuel Cunard issued standing orders to the captains of his ships that "In any case when, in sailing, you are overtaken by thick weather, the most extreme caution is to be exercised and you are not to be actuated by any desire to complete the voyage on schedule, your sole consideration being the safety of your ship."

The Queen Mary's inability to break the speed record on her maiden voyage did not diminish New York City's gala reception for Great Britain's newest superliner. New Yorkers turned out by the tens of thousands to greet the *Queen* as she glided past the Statue of Liberty and up the Hudson River. Hundreds of boats crowded with enthusiastic spectators trailed in the great ship's wake.

Overhead, airplanes swooped and circled around the *Queen*. Several hours before, as she approached the New York coast from the open sea, a DC-2 piloted by famed World War I Ace Eddie Rickenbacker flew to greet the ship. Aboard the plane were newsmen and press photographers, anxious for the first view and first photos of the Queen Mary at sea. The trim twin-engine aircraft flew low over the *Queen*, dropping thousands of white carnations on her decks in greeting. As the Queen Mary sailed majestically up the Hudson, with the skyscrapers of Manhattan as a backdrop and her decks showered with snowy carnations, she looked every inch a queen.

Occasionally, one of the larger excursion steamers pulled close alongside the liner while a band on its upper decks played a musical salute. On the Queen Mary's open Sun Deck, Musical Director Henry Hall conducted the ship's band as it replied with her own signature tune, "Somewhere at Sea," that he had written especially for the *Queen*.

First voyage! A flotilla of boats escorting the RMS Queen Mary *as she departs her Southampton berth on her maiden voyage, May 27, 1936.*

A small flotilla of tugboats gently nudged the Queen Mary into her berth at Pier 90 on the Hudson River. After a special dockside arrival ceremony, Captain Britten and Cunard Chairman Sir Percy Bates led a delegation of Cunard officials to City Hall for a formal welcoming ceremony, where they were greeted by Mayor Fiorello La Guardia. Representing the royal family were the Marquis and Marchioness of Milford Haven.

Curious New Yorkers were allowed aboard the Queen Mary while she was in New York Harbor for a fee of $1 each, which was donated to the seamen's relief fund. Thousands descended upon the *Queen*. Souvenir hunters pocketed anything that was moveable — ashtrays, silverware, brass hardware, plants, even teapots.

First class passengers play deck games on Sports Deck, the highest passenger deck on the ship.

Three months after the maiden voyage, in August 1936, the Queen Mary captured the Blue Riband from the Normandie on her voyage number six, officially completing the Atlantic crossing in 3 days, 23 hours and 57 minutes from Ambrose Lightship to Bishop Rock on the western tip of England. The *Queen's* average speed was 30.63 knots for the nearly 3,000-mile crossing. More than 35 miles per hour (56.73 kmh), it was an incredible speed for a ship grossing more than 80,000 tons.

In order to claim the Blue Riband, a ship had to post the fastest time both ways on the transatlantic route. Since she completed her Southampton-to-New York run in 4 days and 27 minutes at an average speed of 30.14 knots (34.69 mph/55.82 kmh), the Queen Mary surpassed the Normandie's best time by 2 hours and 35 minutes.

As the *Queen* sailed up the Solent River to Southampton, thousands of cheering spectators, alerted by radio of the new record, turned out to cheer. Dozens of steamers, yachts, and pleasure crafts turned out to toot their whistles as they followed the *Queen* to her berth.

But the *Queen's* grasp on the record was brief. The following year, the Normandie posted a westbound crossing of 3 days, 23 hours and 2 minutes at an average speed of 30.58 knots (35.19 mph/56.64 kmh), and an eastbound time of 3 days, 22 hours and 7 minutes at an average speed of 31.2 knots (35.9 mph/57.5 kmh).

Cunard's engineers reviewed the *Queen's* design and decided her performance could be improved with a new propeller design. A set of thirty-ton four-bladed propellers were cast of manganese-bronze, each eighteen feet in diameter. The Queen Mary, her new propellers installed, finally settled her rivalry with the Normandie in August 1938. She steamed to New York in 3 days, 21 hours and 48 minutes at an average speed of 30.99 knots (35.66 mph/57.39 kmh), and returned to England even faster in 3 days, 20 hours and 42 minutes at an average speed of 31.69 knots (36.47 mph/58.67 kmh). The Queen Mary had set a new speed record, which she held for the next fourteen years. Not until 1952 was the *Queen's* record defeated, and then by the SS United States, a much lighter ship which benefited from great advances in post-war technology.

Passengers gathered on the Queen's stern to watch crowded pleasure steamers following the liner as she departs for Cherbourg on the first leg of her maiden voyage.

A regal Queen Mary *passes the Manhattan skyline at the conclusion of her successful maiden voyage on June 1st, 1936. Thousands of steamers and pleasure craft turned out to greet the new "Queen of the Atlantic."*

Bellboys take passengers' dogs for a walk. The Queen Mary *boasted a full-service kennel, complete with lamp post.*

Service—a Cunard Tradition

The Queen Mary's first-class passengers traveled with the assurance that every possible convenience and luxury was available to satisfy their every whim. They could relax and enjoy being pampered and entertained.

Personal service was one of the elements that made the *Queen* a great ship. Stewards and stewardesses were carefully chosen by Cunard, some carrying on a tradition begun by their parents or grandparents, and precisely trained to cater to passengers' needs and demands. The bedroom staff took pride in remembering the likes and dislikes of frequent passengers so that all their requirements could be anticipated on subsequent voyages. Anticipation was, in fact, a key word in the ship's service. The crew was drilled constantly to anticipate passengers' needs and fulfill them without having to be asked.

Dining aboard the Queen Mary was more than just a meal. It was an event, a ritual of culinary elegance. The *Queen*'s cuisine ranked with the very best in the world. Cunard sent its chefs to top restaurants for rigorous training before they were assigned to an ocean liner, where they were expected to be masters of all types of meal preparation. Few, if any, dishes were foreign to the chefs' epicurean repertoire. In fact, so sure was the Master Chef of his ability that he wagered he could prepare anything a passenger might possibly order.

A regular Queen Mary *passenger, Hubert Noble, contemplates a walk around the Promenade Deck.*

When a wealthy Greek asked for couscous, the chef prepared such a delectable steamed wheat-and-lamb stew that he won Grecian accolades from the delighted woman. Southerners from the United States ordered hominy grits for breakfast and enjoyed chicken-fried steak for dinner. The most finicky French gourmet was confident that his discriminating palate would taste French delicacies of uncomparable quality.

On only one occasion did the Queen Mary's chef find himself unable to comply exactly with a diner's request. A Texas oilman jokingly ordered "rattlesnake steak," knowing he would certainly stump the chef. Not to be outdone, the chef served the American two baked eels while waiters shook baby rattles over them. Not exactly what the man requested, but certainly a wager-saving substitute.

The evening meal in first class was a seven-course dinner with all 800 first-class passengers served in the Dining Salon at one sitting. This large-scale event was possible because the Queen Mary's Dining Salon was the largest room ever built within a ship. Measuring 143 feet by 118 feet, the first-class dining room was so extensive that Cunard's first steamship, the Britannia, could have been placed corner to corner in the room with Christopher Columbus' Nina, Pinta, and Santa Maria tucked alongside.

Tea time. Passengers lounging on Promenade Deck are served typical English teacakes.

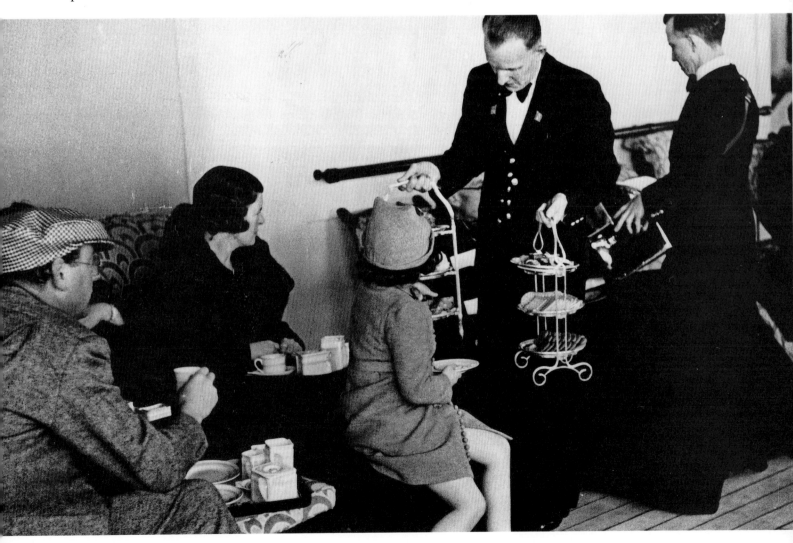

Ship's bellboys line up for a group photograph.

Inspecting some of the Queen Mary's 200,000 pieces of china and glassware. During rough seas, thousands of pieces of crockery were broken and had to be replaced from Southampton stores.

Although several private dining rooms were available, most passengers preferred the main dining room where they could "see and be seen." The world's richest celebrities dined here — Fred Astaire, Greta Garbo, Bob Hope, Gloria Swanson, Elizabeth Taylor, Clark Gable. The Baron and Baroness de Rothschild, the Duke and Duchess of Windsor, and the Vanderbilts all praised the *Queen*'s cuisine.

But the most prestigious seats in the Queen Mary's Dining Salon were at the Captain's table. Seven auspicious passengers were chosen at the beginning of each crossing to dine with the Captain at his table in the center of the grand dining hall. These guests were selected by the Captain himself, with company officials proffering names of VIPs who were aboard.

On one of the ship's voyages, the Captain had filled all but one place at his table. He glanced at the passenger list. Not recognizing any names, the Captain decided to invite the person booked in the *Queen*'s most expensive first-class suite, assuming the man was a prominent figure. He was

A 1936 rendering illustrates the vast amount of foodstuffs carried on the Queen Mary for a single voyage.

Ship's stores are loaded aboard by crane. Normal turnaround time for the Queen Mary *was 24 hours in New York and 48 hours in Southampton. In this time, arriving passengers would disembark, departing passengers would board, and all stores, water, and fuel would be loaded — an incredible feat for so short a time.*

actually a Welsh coal miner who had spent his life's savings to take a "dream vacation" aboard the Queen Mary, a ship he had loved and admired for many years.

The Captain's Steward presented the coal miner with the gilt-edged invitation to dine with the Captain. Unaware of its significance, he angrily told the steward, "I've saved my entire life for this cruise, and I'll be blasted if I'll spend it eating with the crew!" Once the honor was explained to him, he cheerfully dined with the Captain and his other guests, and his voyage became an experience of a lifetime.

To provide enough food for approximately 2,000 passengers and 1,200 crew, an incredible amount of provisions were loaded aboard the Queen Mary before each crossing. The list contained 77,000 pounds of fresh meat, 27,500 pounds of poultry, 11,000 pounds of fresh fish, 50,000 pounds of potatoes, 33,000 pounds of fresh vegetables, 5,000 dozen eggs, 22,000 pounds of flour, 11,000 pounds of sugar, 14,500 gallons of milk, 1,110 boxes of assorted fresh fruit, and 3,000 quarts of ice cream. In addition, the Queen's wine cellar contained more than 15,000 bottles of spirits and fine wine, rivaling the cellars in Europe's finest restaurants.

Queen Elizabeth, wife of King George VI, tours the crew's working alleyway in the Queen Mary.

The Queen's first-class dining salon was comparable to the best of the world's restaurants, but some passengers preferred more exclusive dining. For those discriminating few, the Queen Mary offered the Verandah Grill, a small restaurant on the ship's aft Sun Deck. The most exclusive room on the ship, the Verandah Grill seated only eighty-two first-class passengers at thirty-two tables. Reservations were a must, since an empty seat was rare for dinner, and in most cases, had to be made months in advance.

The Verandah Grill was intended for special á la carte meals during lunch and dinner, and it had its own private bar and kitchen. For the distinction of dining in the Verandah Grill, a patron was charged a £1 cover charge in addition to the price of the meal. At midnight, the tables were removed and the Verandah Grill became the "Starlight Roof" nightclub, offering entertainment and dancing until dawn.

Decorated by Doris Zinkeisen, a well-known British theatrical/film costume and set designer of the 1930s, the Grill featured etched glass panels portraying various musical instruments. The panels, with concealed lights illuminating the edges, decorated the curved center of an elaborate balustrade separating the raised floor from the lower dance floor. Plush burgundy drapes adorned with stitched five-point white stars were drawn back from the tall vertical windows by sashes. The room's jet black carpet created quite a controversy when it was installed. Cunard's management thought it was too "modish," but the carpet became quite a conversation piece.

Onyx fireplace with its Napoleon marble hearth in the First Class Drawing Room on
Promenade Deck. The large mural over the fireplace, Flower Market, as painted by
Kenneth Shoesmith, ROI.

Rabbi uses yad to point to breastplates protecting sections of the Torah used in the ship's synagogue. The Queen Mary *was the first ship to have a Jewish synagogue included in the original plans.*

Altar of the Second Class Catholic Chapel. The chapel was in the Second Class Library, with the altar normally hidden behind a folding wall. The painting behind the altar is titled Madonna of the Tall Ships.

Largest room ever built on a ship, the Queen's First Class Dining Room *is three decks high, 143 feet long, and 118 wide. The largest piece of artwork on the ship, seen at the far end of the room, is entitled* Merry England *by Philip Connard, RA. It depicts, in tapestry style, English country life.*

In a Cunard publicity photo, first class passengers enjoy a sumptuous dinner in the dining room.

Celebration of Splendor

The interior treatments of the Queen Mary's passenger accommodations evidenced the radical artistic influences of the 1930s. Yet the new-style decor blended tastefully with the conservative touches that subtly reflected a quiet sophistication.

The ship's interior rooms, decorated with a mix of furnishings, wood paneling, carpeting, and artwork to create a desired setting and mood, were viewed with enthusiastic approval by critics and journalists. "The rooms will be perfectly satisfying to the most cosmopolitan conceptions of culture and good taste, at the same time retaining the atmosphere of restfulness and comfort associated with the most dignified English country homes." (Booklet, 1935) "Period styles have been discarded in favor of restrained modernism, with a result of subdued elegance." (The Compass, 1936)

The major element of the *Queen's* decor was wood — fifty-six of the world's finest and rarest woods. In every lounge, public room, and passageway, thin wood veneers were used expertly to create a warm and romantic ambience. Wood was so prevalent that the Queen Mary was often dubbed "the ship of beautiful woods."

First Class passengers in dining room during the Queen's *maiden voyage. Passengers always "dressed" for dinner—3 long gowns for women and tuxedos for men.*

The ship's first-class main entrance was paneled in Masur Birch, cross-banded with plain Birch and trimmed in English Elm Burr dado. Light and dark Peroba with Maple Burr panels lined the first-class restaurant. The ship's main staircase was paneled in White English Mottled Ash, with English Elm Burr dado and columns. Promenade Deck's first-class shopping center sported Chestnut-Oak walls, cross-banded with plain Oak, and floor-to-ceiling pillars paneled with English Elm Burr. Mostly popular decorative woods were used in the rooms and hallways, but some rare and little-known woods were also utilized, such as Makore (African Cherry), Acero, Angelim, Avodirbe, Black bean, Bubinga, Corbaril, Ebony, Maidu, Padouk, Synara, Thuya, and Zebrano.

To complement the lavish wood veneers, Cunard hired a team of more than thirty artists and sculptors to decorate the *Queen's* passenger compartments. Notable among the group was Doris Zinkeisen, interior designer of the Verandah Grill, who also painted a thirty-foot mural for the room. Her sister, Anna, was commissioned to create four panels for the ballroom, for which she chose the theme "The Four Seasons."

The Main Lounge on Promenade Deck, one of the most beautiful rooms in the ship, was the social and recreation center for first-class passengers. During the day, organ recitals or performances by the ship's orchestra filled the lounge with music, and tea was served promptly at 4 p.m. In the evening, the lounge featured bingo or horse-racing games.

One of the pierced and carved screens by James Woodford for the Smoking Room, Promenade Deck.

Although the Queen Mary had a ballroom, the Main Lounge was used occasionally for dancing. Men in tuxedoes and women in formal gowns danced their way romantically across the Atlantic.

Second- or third-class passengers were allowed in the Main Lounge on Sunday morning when the Captain performed a non-denominational church service open to all. The Queen Mary was well equipped to fill the needs of her passengers in all classes. Besides the Captain's Sunday service in the Main Lounge, the ship incorporated two Catholic chapels and a Jewish synagogue and held an Anglican service. Additional space was provided as needed for any religious service required by passengers.

A voyage on the Queen Mary was akin to staying in the most luxurious hotel in any of the world's greatest cities. Indeed, the *Queen* was herself a floating city. The size of the great ship caused famed British actress Beatrice Lillie to exclaim, "When does this place get to England?"

From the moment they boarded the Queen Mary, passengers were treated like royalty. Bags and trunks were whisked by baggage handlers to passengers' accommodations while bellboys escorted them to their staterooms or suites. A standard first-class stateroom on the *Queen* was, and is, much larger than the cabins offered on contemporary cruise ships. Each stateroom contained two comfortable single beds, a writing desk, and a small table with overstuffed chairs. Each first-class stateroom also had a private bathroom containing a tub with shower and a sink. The bathtub featured hot and cold running salt water and fresh water, which served two purposes. Firstly, since the *Queen* carried all fresh water in tanks, it helped to conserve water. And, secondly, in the 1930s, salt water was considered to be very therapeutic and many people enjoyed taking a saltwater bath.

The Queen Mary's gardener oversees a newly arrived batch of plants. The ship's flower shop supplied thousands of potted plants, greenery, and assorted flowers for varied areas of the ship.

The walls surrounding the tubs were formica, a new and expensive material in 1936 that equates to decorating with marble today. Some towel racks were electrically heated so passengers had hot towels with which to dry themselves after baths. If a passenger needed assistance while in the bathroom, he or she could reach for a small panel near the tub that contained two buttons — red to call a steward and green to summon a stewardess. The ship's wealthy passengers were accustomed to servants helping them with their baths, but many of the *Queen*'s less experienced passengers were understandably shocked and embarrassed when they accidentally pushed the wrong button.

the Mermaid Bar on the starboard side of Promenade Deck was a popular rendezvous for second class passengers.

A third class cabin was small, but a big step up from the accommodations on most Atlantic steamships of the day.

The Suite

The most luxurious and expensive way to travel on the Queen Mary was in a first-class suite. Suites usually consisted of at least four rooms and a luggage closet, and came in several sizes ranging from one master bedroom with two smaller bedrooms to two master bedrooms with four smaller bedrooms. Each suite was magnificently furnished and decorated. The master bedroom featured a large marquetry panel, handcrafted of inlaid wood, over the beds. Artists used various hues of the fifty-six types of wood utilized throughout the ship's decor for the panels.

The centerpiece of each suite was the sitting room, a spacious parlor furnished in plush overstuffed sofas and chairs. Decorated with paintings, handmade carpets, and ceramic sculptures, each sitting room was unique and exquisite. The room usually contained an electric fireplace, over which hung a peach-glass plate mirror. Ostensibly, during inclement weather, when the ship rolled and the passengers were queasy and pale, one glance in the tinted peach-glass mirror at their rosy cheeks would give them a psychological boost.

Included with each suite was at least one maid's room, for passengers who would not consider traveling without personal servants. Of course, these small bedrooms were also perfect for families with children.

Continuing the tradition of unquestioned personal service, Cunard did everything possible to accommodate the tastes of the Queen Mary's first-class passengers. Favored passengers who requested color and furnishing modifications to their suites were supplied with whatever they wished.

For example, the Duke and Duchess of Windsor always booked number M-58 on Main Deck, a three-room suite. The Duchess was fond of electric blues and greens, and the suite was decorated especially for her in those colors before each voyage. On one occasion, the Duchess reportedly asked that all the furnishings be changed — in mid-Atlantic. Dutiful stewards immediately removed the suite's furniture, scrambling to replace it with furnishings more to the Duchess' liking.

Little did anyone know that soon all the Queen Mary's elegant suites and spacious staterooms would be transformed into soldiers' quarters, and the pride of Great Britain would become the bane of the Nazi hierarchy.

For those passengers who could afford a little extra, there were 26 First class suites, ranging from three to twenty rooms.

Opposite Page:
First Class passenger uses convenient telephone in her cabin. Through radio-telephone connections, Queen Mary passengers could call anywhere in the world while at sea. The ship had more than 600 telephones, keeping several operators busy full-time.

*Many of the suites had spacious
sitting rooms that doubled
as private dining rooms.*

*A first class stateroom was large and lavishly decorated with wood paneling and
artwork. Each stateroom has its own electric heater, fan, and air louvers.*

Stewards at work cleaning the main lounge on Promenade Deck—a major center of activity for first class passengers. Towering over the onyx fireplace is a beautiful gesso panel titled Unicorns in Battle *by Gilbert Bayes and Alfred Oakley.*

Playroom attendant has toys all lined up and ready for children in the Second Class Playroom.

Playful mural painted by George Ramon for the First Class Children's Playroom.

in the First Class Playroom wait patiently for children to
. Besides hundreds of toys, dolls, and games, the playroom
projection room where children could watch cartoons.

A LIST OF FAMOUS PASSENGERS

Politicians/Statesmen

Winston Churchill
Anthony Eden, British Foreign Minister
General Dwight D. Eisenhower
Walter S. Gifford, American Ambassador
    in London

Royalty/Socialites

Baron and Baroness Elie de Rothschild
King Faisal II of Iraq
Sir Cedric Hardwicke and valet
Lady Hardwicke and maid
Master E. C. Hardwicke
Duke and Duchess of Windsor

Movie Stars

Don Ameche
Annabella
George Arliss
Mr. and Mrs. Fred Astaire
    and maid
Lionel Barrymore
Constance Bennett
Joe E. Brown
Eddie Cantor
Mr. and Mrs. Charles M.
    Chaplin and maid
Mr. and Mrs. Gary Cooper
Marian Davies
Delores Del Rio
Marlene Dietrich
Douglas Fairbanks Jr.
Douglas Fairbanks Sr.
Gracie Fields
Greta Garbo
Bonita Granville
Oliver Hardy
Hildegarde

Men and Women of Letters

Noel Coward
Hedda Hopper
W. Somerset Maugham
J. B. Priestly
Earl Wilson

Tycoons and Financiers

Henry Ford Jr.
Huntington Hartford
Aristotle S. Onassis
Michael Todd
Jack Wrather

Movie Stars

Bob Hope
Leslie Howard
Stan Laurel
Gertrude Lawrence
Liberace
Beatrice Lillie
Margaret Lockwood
Raymond Massey
Johnny Mathis
Adolphe Menjou
Colleen Moore
David Niven
Jack Oakie
Merle Oberon
Bert Parks
Mary Pickford
Lily Pons
Paul Robeson
Alexis Smith
Robert Stack
Gloria Swanson
Sylvia Sydney
Elizabeth Taylor
Robert Taylor
Spencer Tracy
Sophie Tucker
Johnny Weissmuller
Anna May Wong
Loretta Young
Robert Young
Roland Young

Mary Pickford sits at the dressing table in her suite during a crossing in 1937.

Famous actor Lionel Barrymore in the First Class Main Lounge.

Previous Page:
Namesakes of the greatest ocean liners ever built are shown in this photograph taken at Pincess Anne's christening. From left to right: Queen Mary, *Queen Elizabeth II, and* Queen Elizabeth, *the Queen Mother.*

Previous Page:
Famous playwright Noel Coward pauses during an afternoon stroll on Sports Deck in 1936.

Actress Marian Davies chats on a ship's telephone.

Comedian Buster Keaton struggles to remove his baggage from the bottom of the pile while his wife looks away in mock disgust.

Actor Leslie Howard and his wife look over the ship's passenger list.

Comedians Stan Laurel and Oliver Hardy mug for the ship's photographer.

A crew member instructs passengers in the proper fitting of life preservers on the Queen Mary's maiden voyage. Lifeboat drill was performed during the first full day of every voyage.

The Queen Mary's Sun Deck is more than 720 feet long—3 longer than many modern-day cruise ships. Lifeboats are secured on their davits high above the deck.

Maiden-voyage passengers enjoy a friendly game of quoits.

Opposite Page:
For passengers wishing to stay in shape during the voyage, the liner had gymnasiums stocked with exercise and athletic equipment. Here, two gentlemen try out the mechanical horses.

As the Queen Mary *sets sail on her maiden voyage on May 27, 1936, the ships's orchestra plays on the vessel's stern.*

A *forward lookout stands near the ship's bell in the foc'sle, the forwardmost point of the ship's bow.*

Commodore James Bissett relaxes in his day-room.

Tugboats strain to guide the Queen Mary *downriver as she heads for the open sea from the John Brown Shipyard on March 24, 1936.*

Faster than most warships, the Queen Mary *usually traveled alone without protection. She relied on secrecy and her great speed to elude enemy ships and planes. The sight of the great liner slipping silently and swiftly across the seas in her camouflage paint earned her the nickname* The Gray Ghost.

THE QUEEN

GOES TO WAR

The second class bar on Main Deck was converted into a dispensary during troopship days.

Chapter III

The summer of 1939 found the Queen Mary at the height of her success. All of Cunard's expectations for the giant ship had come true: she was big, she was safe, and she was fast; best of all, she was profitable.

But events in Europe soon cut short the *Queen*'s glamorous career and set her on a new course—a course that would take the Queen Mary to seas and ports her builders had never dreamed she would visit — in a role dictated by the grim necessities of war.

For months, the likelihood of war increased as the British government engaged in a hopeless attempt to appease Adolf Hitler's territorial demands. All pretense at negotiation finally ended, however, when Nazi forces launched a surprise invasion of Poland in September 1939.

The Queen Mary departed on her last peacetime voyage on August 30, two days before the German attack. As Nazi troops poured into Poland, the *Queen* was in mid-Atlantic bound for New York. The clouds of war had been gathering for some time, and thousands of people were leaving Europe before hostilities broke out. Filled to overflowing, the Queen Mary carried a record number of passengers: 2,329. Making the voyage were comedian Bob Hope and his wife. "Delores and I were in Paris when we were ordered home," he recalls. "We made London in time to catch the Queen Mary's last trip. She was carrying the maximum. Everyone she could crowd. People were actually sleeping in the passageways. I couldn't believe there would be a war, and I said so. Then England declared war."

It was nearly midnight on September 2 when Commodore R. B. Irving received a coded message from the Admiralty ordering him to put the Queen Mary on full war alert, and to take every precaution to ensure the liner's safe arrival in New York. The message also warned him to be on the alert for enemy submarines.

Immediately, Commodore Irving ordered the helmsman to steer a zig-zag course and posted additional lookouts to watch for enemy vessels or aircraft. Crewmen were sent to the staterooms and cabins to paint the ship's portholes black. The *Queen*'s running and deck lights were turned off, and the great ship raced in complete darkness for the safety of New York Harbor. The next morning, the passengers listened as the ship's public address system broadcast Prime Minister Neville Chamberlain's fateful message, ". . . this nation is at war with Germany."

With war now official, the Queen Mary was a prime target for Nazi submarines. Worried passengers cast fearful glances at the dark seas where, at any moment, a lurking U-boat could launch a deadly attack. The *Queen*'s only defense being her speed, she steamed toward New York at nearly 30 knots. Anxious passengers breathed a sigh of relief when she sailed safely into New York Harbor on September 4, and docked at Pier 90. In the berth next to the *Queen* was her transatlantic rival, the Normandie, also taking refuge from the enemy.

Another ship was not as fortunate. Less than ten hours after Chamberlain's proclamation of war, German submarine U-30 torpedoed the British liner Athenia off the coast of Scotland. One hundred and twelve passengers, including twenty-eight Americans, lost their lives in the first marine casualty of World War II.

A soldier's original snapshot shows members of the gun crew posing with ammunition for one of the five 40-mm anti-aircraft guns mounted on the Queen Mary.

"Wrens" (Women's Royal Naval Service) working in Communication Office.

Previous Page:
The Queen Mary rests between voyages at Cunard Pier 90 in New York. Also berthed are the Britannic and the second Mauretania.

Most of the Queen's crew soon returned to England and other war-related duties, leaving a small maintenance crew to look after the ship. Since she was a major target for Nazi saboteurs, a twenty-four-hour military guard was placed around the vessel.

On March 7, 1940, the Queen Mary received a surprise visit from her sistership, the Queen Elizabeth. The partially finished Elizabeth was in the John Brown & Company shipyard at Clydebank, Scotland, when Britain declared war, well within range of German bombers from the continent. She left Scotland on March 2, supposedly for sea trials and a short voyage to Southampton. Even her crew was unaware of the true nature of the voyage they were beginning — they were told to pack just enough clothing for the short trip to Southampton.

When the Elizabeth reached the sea, her captain opened sealed orders from the Admiralty commanding him to take the ship immediately and directly to New York, even though the Queen Elizabeth had had no formal sea trials to test her engines, her operating systems, or her crew. Under such conditions, the voyage to America would be hazardous. She secretly crossed the Atlantic without incident, however, and upon arriving in New York, the Elizabeth tied up alongside the Mary. They were a spectacular sight, both now painted in wartime gray; the Normandie, in striking contrast, still wore her peacetime colors.

In England, great controversy waged about the use of the giant passenger liners. Many Admiralty and government authorities felt the Queens were too vulnerable to be used as troopships. Some even suggested that they be sold to raise money for the war effort. But all soon realized that the sisterships were much too valuable as transports to be wasted.

The situation in England had become critical. The British army was nearly destroyed at Dunkirk, and Hitler's powerful armies were poised on the continent, ready to pounce on the island at the Führer's command.

The Queen Mary was quickly drafted into war service, her size and usefulness as a troop transport outweighing the danger. On March 21, 1940, the gray Queen silently slipped down the Hudson to the open sea and turned south. Her departure and destination were top secret.

As she sped away from New York, the Queen Mary was undergoing unusual alterations. The Queen had already been camouflaged with a coat of gray paint, and her 2½-foot-high name obliterated. Soon she would be known by the apt nom de guerre of the Grey Ghost, scourge of the Nazi U-boats. Racing across the seas or slipping silently in and out of the fog, no sooner was her profile sighted by enemy vessels than she seemed to magically disappear.

The fastest ship afloat, the Queen Mary could race at more than 30 knots (34.5 mph/55.6 kmh) and maintain that incredible speed for thousands of miles. In the early days of the war, she was actually faster than German torpedoes.

After a refueling stop in Cape Town, South Africa, the *Queen* sailed for Sydney, Australia, where her luxurious fittings were removed and she was converted into a troopship capable of transporting 5,000 soldiers.

A special sound detection sonar was installed to allow the ship to pinpoint submerged enemy submarines so she could maneuver to avoid them. Unfortunately, the device proved ineffective. The *Queen*'s massive propellers were too noisy for the sonar system to operate properly.

Anti-aircraft machine guns were mounted in strategic locations on the upper decks, and a small six-inch gun was anchored to the Queen Mary's stern. Although useless against a concerted attack by submarine, aircraft or warship, the six-inch armament would be handy against a small vessel or reconnaissance aircraft. To protect her from magnetic mines, an electronic degaussing, or demagnetizing, strip was attached to the ship's hull to repel underwater explosives.

When the conversion was complete, 5,000 Australian troops boarded and the Queen Mary began her first voyage as a troop carrier.

Faced with the possibility of invasion, Great Britain needed every soldier available in her far-reaching commonwealth. Thus, on the morning of May 4, 1940, the *Queen* sailed with the liners Aquitania, Mauretania, Empress of Japan, Empress of Canada, and Empress of Britain, also recently converted to troopships, escorted by a group of warships. The liners called at Fremantle, Australia, for supplies and additional troops, then sailed for Scotland with refueling stops at Cape Town, Simonstown, and Freetown.

On the same day the Queen Mary dropped anchor in Gourlock, Scotland, war-torn France appealed to Hitler for an armistice. Allied troops evacuated Norway, Italy declared war on England, and Britain was desperately short of manpower and material.

Following a stay of thirteen days in the Firth of Clyde, the Queen Mary was ordered to Singapore for much-needed drydocking. Sailing from Scotland on June 29, 1940, she completed the 14,000-mile voyage without mishap and was placed in Singapore's giant drydock on August 5. The next 41 days were filled with frantic activity as workmen cleaned the ship's hull, and mechanics and engineers overhauled her engines, boilers, and steering mechanisms. Later, in Sydney, a set of paravanes was attached to

The three largest passenger liners ever built, at berth in New York in March, 1940. Left to right are the Normandie, Queen Mary, and the Queen Elizabeth with her hull paint still missing from her top secret dash across the Atlantic.

the *Queen's* bow to augment the degaussing strips. Consisting of two floating devices shaped like torpedoes, the paravanes were towed from the ship's bow. As the ship moved through the water, they spread out on either side of the vessel. The paravanes' towing cables intercepted any mines along the ship's course and cut their anchor lines, causing the mines to bob to the surface where they could be destroyed by gunfire from the *Queen's* decks.

When the Italian army invaded Egypt on September 14, 1940, British military leaders were shocked. Suddenly, the entire direction of the war changed. With the Italians in North Africa, the vital Suez Canal was in danger of being captured by the Axis powers.

After the Italian invasion of Africa, the Queen Elizabeth, still docked in New York Harbor, was prepared for war service. She sailed for Singapore for conversion and continued to Sydney for final fitting out as a troopship.

The Queen Mary met her bigger sister at sea for the first time in April 1941 off the Australian coast at Sydney Head. The two giant sisterships sailed together on April 9, 1941, carrying a combined troop complement of 10,000 New Zealand and Australian soldiers. On this voyage, the *Queens* were in convoy with the Cunarder Mauretania. For the remainder of 1941, the Queen Mary made Sydney her home port and continued to ferry troops and supplies to the Middle East.

Although the danger to the *Queen* from enemy aircraft or submarines was great, temperature was an even greater threat on the Sydney-to-Suez voyages. Designed to ply the cold North Atlantic, the Queen Mary had not been equipped with adequate air-conditioning for the hot climates through which she was now sailing. Allied troops and German prisoners suffered horribly from the suffocating heat below decks. Harry Grattidge, the *Queen's* Staff Captain on many of these voyages, often assisted the ship's sole chaplain in the solemn task of burying the dead at sea. In his book, *Captain of the Queen,* he writes, "Almost every four hours came news of another death. Both the Bo'sun and the Deck Storekeeper, who prepare bodies for a burial, were almost rushed off their feet . . . four times a day I was forced to intone the gravest words that a ship's officer can utter: 'Man that is born of woman has but a short time to live' . . ."

Japan's surprise attack on Pearl Harbor on December 7, 1941, and the destruction of the U.S. Pacific fleet forced drastic changes in British war strategy. Thus far, British shipping vessels had sailed the Pacific and southern seas in virtual safety, the only danger being a chance encounter with a long-range German warship or submarine. Japan's entry into the

Thousands of soldiers crowd the bow of the ship during lifeboat drill. Although the Queen *carried extra lifeboats and dozens of inflatable rafts, her sinking could have resulted in thousands of fatalities.*

war on the side of the Axis coalition changed that. The British Pacific colonies, including Singapore, were immediately endangered. Even Australia, weakened by the great number of troops sent to other war fronts, was in danger of invasion by Japanese armies.

Soon after the attack on Pearl Harbor, the Queen Mary was turned over to American military commanders. She remained under the command of her British captain and crew, but her duties and destinations were determined by American authorities.

The *Queen* was moved to the Boston Navy Yard for an extensive refitting. Her troop capacity was increased to 8,200, with metal standee berths being erected in drawing rooms, in lounges, and even in drained swimming pools.

May 1942. Photo shows some defensive armament along the port side of the Queen Mary.

As the Queen Mary *approached dangerous coastlines, British or American aircraft meet the ship to offer air support and submarine protection.*

Gun crews rush to stations "on the double" during an exercise. Guns were manned by both British and American gunners.

View of the Queen Mary *at full speed, taken from the bridge of the British cruiser HMS* Scylla *in May 1943. On board the* Queen *was Prime Minister Winston Churchill and his party, enroute to New York and Washington to meet with President Roosevelt.*

The *Queen's* armament was also improved. Five 40mm double-barreled cannons were installed: two on the bow, two on the stern, and one above the bridge. Twenty-four 20mm guns were mounted in strategic positions on the *Queen's* upper decks. Six three-inch guns augmented the six-inch cannon and the many .50- and .30-caliber machine guns already aboard. Near the after funnel (smokestack), four sets of anti-aircraft rocket launchers were installed. Many years later, a member of the gun crew recalled, "The pillar boxes had twin cradles for 20 rockets each which were fired electrically and were adapted for high-angle and low-angle targets."

Refitted and newly armed, the Queen Mary embarked 8,398 soldiers and sailed northeast out of Boston on February 18, 1942. As soon as she was out of sight of land, the *Queen* turned sharply south, proceeding to Trinidad. Her destination was Sydney, where her passengers and cargo (artillerymen and ordnance supplies) were sorely needed.

As the Queen Mary neared Trinidad, heavy U-boat activity was reported and she was rerouted to Key West. While in Florida, the *Queen* took on fuel, provisions, and a new captain. Ship's Captain John Townley, having reached mandatory retirement age, was replaced by James Bisset.

Leaving Key West, Captain Bisset steered the *Queen* on a winding course through the Caribbean, finally traversing the narrow Anegada Passage to the open sea. Less than a half-hour later, the *Queen's* radioman intercepted a distress signal from a torpedoed steamer ten miles astern of the liner's course. The enemy was near.

Winter in the North Atlantic. The Gray Ghost *plows through heavy seas. A wave brakes over the top of the ship's bridge, which is 110 feet above the waterline.*

The presence of the Axis powers was also felt in Rio de Janeiro. While the *Queen* refueled and replenished her stores, Axis spies plotted to destroy her. Using a radio hidden in the hills above the port, they signalled the *Queen*'s course and departure time to their comrades just minutes before being captured by Allied authorities. Captain Bisset, warned that her departure time had been revealed to the enemy, finished refueling, then sailed several hours early.

The *Queen* got safely away, but a tanker leaving Rio at her scheduled departure time was torpedoed by a German submarine waiting outside the harbor. So certain were the Axis authorities of the Queen Mary's destruction that one Italian radio station actually reported she had been sunk. On board the *Queen*, safely at sea, a radioman rushed onto the bridge and exclaimed, "Sir, I've just received a radio message that we have been torpedoed and sunk." Captain Bisset calmly replied, "Well, don't tell the passengers. We wouldn't want to alarm them."

Always vulnerable to torpedo attacks, the Queen Mary kept moving at all times. During one return crossing to New York, a lifeboat from a torpedoed steamer was sighted. Knowing that a submarine could be waiting nearby, Captain Bisset did not stop to rescue the survivors, but signaled to them that he would radio their position to rescue vessels. One of the survivors was the son of the Queen Mary's Chief Purser. As the ship raced away, leaving him stranded, he uttered some colorful words for his father. Thanks to the *Queen*'s message, however, the lifeboat occupants were rescued the next day by an American vessel.

In late 1942, the Queen Mary was once again traveling her accustomed route on the North Atlantic. A massive troop buildup had begun, and the *Queen* was needed to transport American and Canadian soldiers to England. To expedite the buildup, American and British military leaders considered increasing both of the *Queens'* troop capacity to 10,000 each. American General George C. Marshall, worried about the risk of losing so many men if either ship were torpedoed, consulted with Prime Minister Winston Churchill, who told him that if it could shorten the war by even one day, the risk was worth taking. Marshall decided to pay a personal visit to the Queen Mary and see for himself the potential problems of carrying 10,000 troops.

The biggest problem of transporting so many men, explained Staff Captain Harry Grattidge, was crossing the Holland Tunnel beneath the Hudson River. So fully loaded, the ship's keel would be very near the top of the tunnel. If the men lined the ship's side as they normally did, the *Queen* would list, increasing her draft, and she would most likely strike the tunnel. General Marshall solved the problem in a unique manner. As the ship neared the tunnel, the vessel's army commander shouted into the public address system, "All troops, attention!" While the Queen Mary sailed safely over the tunnel, her military personnel stood perfectly still.

Twice, with Winston Churchill aboard, the *Queen* put into Halifax Harbor in Nova Scotia to embark Canadian soldiers bound for the front lines. As on all transatlantic voyages, she traveled alone, without escort. For most warships to accompany the swift *Queen*, she would have had to travel at reduced speed, a real danger in submarine-infested waters. So, the *Queen* would leave New York with protective destoyers and aircraft following her as far as they could. When she arrived off the coast of Scotland, she would again be met by protective aircraft and warships as she approached the coastline.

Miraculously, the *Queen* encountered only one serious accident during the war, in October 1942. Approaching the coast of Scotland, with 10,000 American troops aboard, the Queen Mary was met by a small flotilla of destroyers equipped to defend the liner from submarine attack, if necessary. Leading the flotilla was the 4,290-ton British anti-aircraft cruiser HMS Curacoa. Procedure called for the destroyers to form a protective cordon around the *Queen*, and the Curacoa, armed with heavy anti-aircraft guns, remained near in case enemy aircraft were spotted.

Suddenly, before anyone on either ship realized the danger, the Queen Mary, still on a zig-zag course, and the Curacoa converged at high speed. The force of the giant liner striking the 450-foot-long warship 150 feet forward of the cruiser's stern spun the Curacoa broadside to the *Queen's* massive bow. Like a hot knife slicing through butter, the Queen Mary cut the Curacoa in half, plowing straight through the stricken cruiser.

Many of the Curacoa's crew died instantly, trapped below decks by the onslaught of cold seawater. Two crewmen, unable to escape through the ship's regular passages, crawled into a hatch leading into one of the vessel's funnels. Making their way through the narrow passage and out onto the

Dramatic photograph of the burning forward section of the light cruiser, H.M.S. Curacoa, after being struck by the Queen Mary.

Opposite Page:
The crushed bow of the Queen Mary *after collision with the cruiser HMS* Curacoa. *Photo was taken during repairs in drydock at Boston Harbor.*

side of the foundering ship, they slid down the ship's hull into the water along with dozens of their comrades.

On the upper decks of the *Queen*, horrified soldiers and crewmen watched as the two halves of the Curacoa bobbed astern, sinking rapidly. Some quick-thinking soldiers hurled life preservers into the sea, hoping to aid the men in the water. The two halves of the Curacoa sank in less than five minutes.

On the bridge of the Queen Mary, Captain Cyril Illingworth was faced with a difficult decision. Should he stop and lower lifeboats to save the seamen struggling in the water? On board the Queen Mary were 10,000 soldiers whose safety depended on him, and they were sailing in a favorite sea-lair of Nazi U-boats. Captain Illingworth made the only decision he could. The *Queen* sailed on, but sent a radio message to the other vessels to rescue the Curacoa survivors.

Captain Illingworth was faced with another serious question. How badly damaged was the Queen Mary? He knew the *Queen* could not have cut through an armor-plated cruiser without sustaining serious damage to her bow. Illingworth sent Staff Captain Grattidge forward to inspect the damage, and, as a safety precaution, reduced the liner's speed.

When Grattidge arrived on the scene, he was relieved. The *Queen* had a gaping hole in her bow, but the shattered steel plates had folded back into

Although gambling was strictly forbidden aboard, a group of American soldiers takes time out for their favorite pastime using metal "standee berths" (pictured here). With as little as 18 inches of clearance between berths, it was possible to bunk 21 soldiers in a first class cabin intended for two passengers.

American army officers learn the quiet pleasures of English tea time in the ship's officers' wardroom.

Soldiers form "chow line" in the First Class Dining Room. Outfitted with cafeteria-style tables and benches, the elegant room still retains the aura of its former glory. Soldiers were fed only two meals a day, but were encouraged to carryout food for between-meal snacks.

the hole, partially closing it. Water surged in and out of the hole, but the ship's forward collision bulkhead was holding. If the bulkhead had been smashed by the crash or the pounding of the incoming waves, the ship would not have survived. Grattidge immediately ordered reinforcement of the bulkhead, and the Queen Mary continued on to Gourock, Scotland, at half speed. With no facilities available to repair the damaged bow plates, workmen had to make temporary repairs. Tons of cement were poured into the hole to seal it. The *Queen* then sailed to the Boston Naval Yard for permanent repairs.

Even though the nearby destroyers moved in quickly to rescue the Curacoa's crew, loss of life was great. Of the more than 400 officers and men aboard, 338 died. The official investigation produced contradictory findings. At first, responsibility for the collision was determined to lay with the Captain of the Curacoa, reasoning that the warship should have stayed clear of the Queen Mary. Later, the final settlement apportioned two-thirds of the responsibility to the Curacoa and one-third to the Queen Mary. It was a decision that cost Cunard thousands of pounds in compensation for damages.

The collision was one of the war's best-kept secrets. Fearful that the Axis powers would use the incident for propaganda purposes, the Allies clamped a tight security lid on all details of the accident until after the war.

The Allied need for more soldiers and supplies in Great Britain was insatiable. To fulfill this demand, the Queen Mary's troop-carrying capabilities were once again increased — to 15,000. For the first time in history, an entire division was transported on a single ship. The Queen Mary set a record on July 25, 1943, sailing from New York to Gourock with 15,740 passengers and a crew of 943 aboard, a total of 16,683 persons. The record stands today as the greatest number of people ever embarked on a ship for any voyage.

The Queen Mary and her sistership, the Queen Elizabeth, were both plying the transatlantic route carrying 15,000 troops each in summer and 10,000 in winter. The *Queen's* schedule was almost as regular as it had been before the war. She would arrive in New York Harbor in the afternoon, embark troops, refuel and load supplies, then sail with the morning tide — all in less than ninety-six hours, with the 15,000 troops embarking in less than twelve hours. Upon awakening, sleepy-eyed New Yorkers would gaze at the *Queen's* empty berth and wonder if they had merely dreamed her the night before.

It was little wonder that the Queen Mary was known as the *Grey Ghost*. She sailed into New York Harbor unannounced and departed without warning, slipping silently away in the early morning mists.

During her numerous New York-to-Gourock voyages, the *Queen* served double duty. On the westbound crossing, she carried thousands of German prisoners of war to detention centers in the United States. Wounded soldiers cared for by the ship's expert hospital staff were also sent home on the *Queen*.

Former Second Class Children's Playroom takes on new role as the Royal Air Force's orderly room.

Loaded down with as many as she can carry, the Queen Mary sets out on another dangerous voyage across the Atlantic. The liner would often carry more than 15,000 troops on a single crossing, and still holds the record for the most people ever carried on a ship (16,683).

Gin Rummy Aboard Ship *by Robert Bizinsky. This pen and ink drawing is one of many created during a 1942 Queen Mary voyage by the famous post-impressionist artist. As an American soldier, Bizinsky served in England, North Africa, and the Middle East. His wartime drawings are a sensitive look into the personal side of men at war.*

OCEAN DAILY NEWS

EDITOR: 1ST. LIEUT. RALPH BLANCHARD

OFFICE: STUDIO, PROMENADE DECK

THURSDAY, MARCH 19, 1942

ASST. EDITOR: PVT. JAMES C. KURZ

No. 21.

GENERAL MacARTHUR NOW IN AUSTRALIA TO COMMAND LAND, SEA, AIR FORCES OF ALLIES AT REQUEST OF AUSTRALIAN GOVERNMENT

Major-General Wainwright Commands Philippines

General Douglas MacArthur has arrived in Australia and will command the Allied Nations' land, sea and air forces in the Anzac area and the Philippines at the request of the Australian Government, according to an announcement made by the War Department in Washington. In his new position General MacArthur will have powers similar to those of General Wavell in India.

Accompanying General MacArthur on his arrival in Australia were Mrs. MacArthur, their son, Major-General Richard Sutherland, Chief of Staff, and Brigadier-General H. H. George of the Air Corps.

Major-General Wainwright was named to succeed General Mac-Arthur in command of the Bataan forces. The announcement made it clear that this in no way means that the Bataan Peninsula is lost. General Wainwright is one of the best students of modern war technique.

This new appointment is a tribute to General MacArthur's heroic resistance which has fired the imagination of the whole free world. With a small land force and a few planes he was able to accomplish stupendous deeds. He has wiped out whole regiments of Japanese troops.

General MacArthur was given command of the US Army in the Far East last July. He is years old and was the youngest ever had up to the time of retirement in 1937. The has received 13 decorations for bravery under fire and leading "Rainbow" Division.

Dutch troops have Australia from the take their place in Australian, British troops already

In the raid day the Japs ation bombs is designed causing the raid and elev Jap on the Jap the

GENERAL REDS TIGHTEN HOLD ON 16th GERMAN ARMY

The Russians are drawing the ring of steel tighter around the 16th German Army, trapped in the Staraya Russa sector. Thousands of Germans have been wiped out, and 80 places have been liberated in two weeks.

All attempts by the Germans to send reinforcements have failed. In the last fortnight, 90 German planes, most of them Junkers transports, have been shot down.

Moscow reports a terrific battle for a city in the south west. In an attack, the Russians have taken an important junction. The Russians have laid down an extremely heavy barrage in the Donets Sector.

Many Germans have been killed on the Kalinin front. The Russian German newspaper accounts have strengthened the Russian reports. Switzerland reports that a new cold front exists in Russia. Tanks are frozen solid in the ground. It is 13 degrees below zero in the Crimea.

★ ★ ★
Previous Condition of Servitude!

Lieut. Col. C. H. Cowart, C.O. of the 104th CA Battalion (Sep.), was the branch sales manager for Remington Rand, Inc., at Birmingham, Ala. His territory included Mobile, Ala., Meridan, Miss. and Pensecola, Fla.

Lieut. R. E. Cloud, S-2 of the 104th CA Battalion (Sep.), played no favorites in choosing his work. His selection included selling coke, surveying, junior chemist, bank teller, assistant cashier of the City of Birmingham, Ala., and salesman for the Penn Mutual Life Insurance Co.

Lieut. C. P. Cleveland, Jr., Aide-de-Camp to General Van Volkenburgh, bears a financial background. He graduated in the class of '35 from the Citadel and served as book-keeper for the Citizens & Southern National Bank of South Carolina at Spartanburg, S.C. He later entered the General Financial & Trust in the same city.

1st Lieut. Grady Wright, the ever busy director of the muscle department, toiled for the Fire Insurance Underwriters at Atlanta, Ga.

★ ★ ★
CHESS TOURNAMENT

All men who entered the Chess tournament will report at Prom. Deck, starboard side, aft of the Lounge, at 7.30 tonight.

Draw Capsules From Fishbowl

The drawing of 7,000 capsules from the giant fish bowl took place last night in the third draft of this war. This draft will accomodate those men who registered on February 16. The honor of drawing the first capsule falls to Secretary of war Henry L. Stimson, and Director of selective service, Hershey, will make the speech of the evening. 17½ million men were registered in the first two calls.

Daily Lenten Bible Reading

"The Lord is good, a stronghold in the day of trouble; and he knoweth them that trust in him." Nah. 1:7.

AMERICANS RUSH TO PAY INCOME TAX

Americans are rushing to get their income taxes fully paid early in order that the money can go into the war effort. $1,700,000 was collected in income tax in the first two weeks of this month. This more than doubles the sum paid in the same period last year. In one town in Indiana some 155,000 blanks have been filled in as against 51,300 by this time of last year. $2,700,000,000 in income tax is expected this year.

Speaking of money, President Roosevelt is asking Congress for $17,500,000 for armaments. It is expected that 60,000 planes will be built in 1942 and 120,000 in 1943.

DALTON ANNOUNCES POWER RATIONING

Sir Hugh Dalton, who is in charge of rationing in England, has announced that power consumption in England must be cut. Coal, gas and electricity will all be under the strictest rationing regulations. Dalton says, "Without coal, there can be no arms." 50% of the power consumption is now going into arms production and the people are accepting new rationing gladly.

Clothing, too, will receive a 25% cut. It is believed that this cut in the clothing rations will permit greater space in the ships for arms material.

Indications are that a shortage of wheat may soon exist in England.

AUSTRALIAN MONEY VALUE

For the information of the members of this command, a description of the currency and coins, in more or less common circulation in Australia, is stated below:—

Description	Written Reference	Slang Reference	US Value
Five Pound Note	£5/0/0	Fiver	$16.00
One Pound Note	£1/0/0	Quid	$3.20
Half Pound Note or Ten Shilling Note	£0/10/0 or 10/-	Ten Bob	$1.60
Crown (silver coin)	£0/5/0 or 5/-	Five Bob	$0.80
Two Shilling coin (silver) or Florin	£0/2/0 or 2/-	Two Bob	$0.32
One Shilling coin (silver)	£0/1/0 or 1/-	Bob	$0.16
Six Penny coin (silver)	£0/0/6 or 6d		$0.08
Three Penny coin (silver)	£0/0/3 or 3d		$0.04
One Penny coin (copper)	£0/0/1 or 1d	Copper	$0.013
Half Penny coin (copper)	£0/0/0½ or ½d		$0.0065

In comparing Australian coins with American coins in size, it is noted that the crown is the same size as our silver dollar, the florin is similar in size to our half dollar, and the shilling compares with our quarter, the six pence coin is of the same size as our dime, the three pence coin being smaller, the two copper coins, the penny and half penny, are unusually large for their relative value, the penny is as large as our half dollar, the half penny is the size of our quarter. Arrangements will be made for the conversion of American money into Australian money by members of this command.

The ship's printing presses were used to keep the soldiers aboard informed about world events and everyday events on the Queen. The Ocean Daily News *was printed by an American staff, and each issue was eagerly awaited by news-hungry troops.*

Map shows ports of call visited during the Queen Mary's wartime voyages.

OCEAN DAILY NEWS

EDITORIAL OFFICE : PICCADILLY CIRCUS, PROMENADE DECK

No. 8

MONDAY, JANUARY 4, 1943

ONE PENNY

Hitler Threatens His Retreating Troops

WARNS OF REPRISALS AGAINST FAMILIES

LONDON, SUNDAY.

Driven to desperate measures by the continued advances of the Red Army, Hitler has now threatened to have shot by their own comrades any of his troops who retreat or try to surrender, and has added a warning that reprisals will also be taken against their families.

These threats were made by the German Commander on the Central Russian front during the battle for Velikie Luki, the most important German base in this sector.

Battered by the Russian troops and threatened by their own leaders, the Nazis fought furiously but unavailingly. The town fell to the Red A[...] fiercest batt[...] war, and th[...] supply colum[...] their way t[...] streets.

Latest Mo[...] state that th[...] vancing west[...] are within 15[...] the Leningrad[...] railway.

If this offens[...] cessfully, the [...] cation link be[...] and the Cent[...] seriously threat[...]

Further repo[...] position of the [...] in the Rzhev sa[...] the Don and V[...] more serious.

In the Lowe[...] Red Army is w[...] Simienskya. It [...] that the German[...] early last summe[...] attack on Stalin[...] sector the Russi[...] the capture of [...] Volga—Black S[...] miles from Koteln[...]

After bitter [...] Caucasus, Sovie[...] pied a di[...] [...] [...]ve made rapid [...] ea of the Kalmu[...] een the Caspian [...] [...]ucasus.

BRITISH RAID BEHIND ENEMY LINES

The story has now been published of how, in the early days of the battle of El Alamein last November, two squadrons of light Britis[...]

NAZI DIPLOMATS SACKED

The German ambassadors to Japan, Spain and Sweden, have been replaced. These changes do not seem to be due to personal reasons, but appear to reflect Hitler's anger at the state of German relations with these countries.

Japan has failed to co-ordinate with Germany and Italy, and has refused to take part in the war against Russia.

Spain has refused to take any action which might bring her into conflict with the Allied nations.

Sweden has refused any further credits to Germany until June next and made deliveries to Germany dependent on G[...]

Belgian Judges' Strike Succeeds

The strike of over a thousand Belgian judges and magistrates, reported in the *Ocean Daily News*, has been successful.

The strike arose because the Belgian Supreme Court declared certain German decrees illegal. The members of the Court were imprisoned, and all their fellow judges struck work in sympathy. The judicial system came to a complete standstill, and the Germans had to rescind several of the decrees made.

This is the third success[...]

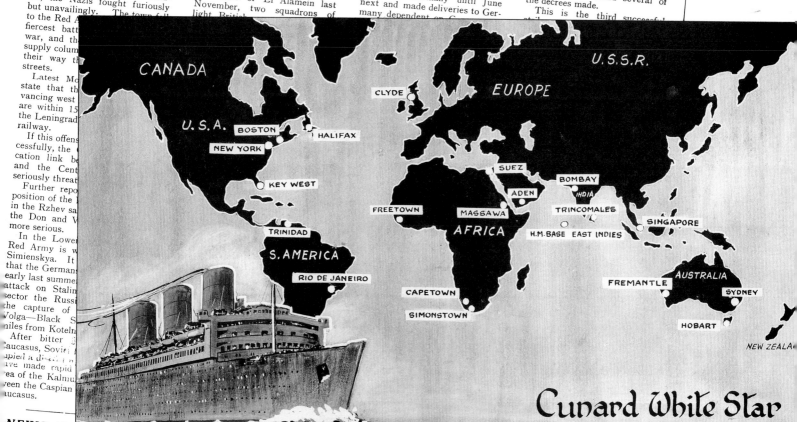

Cunard White Star

WARTIME VOYAGES.

NEW YORK, TRINIDAD, CAPETOWN, FREMANTLE, SYDNEY.	SYDNEY, SINGAPORE, FREMANTLE, SYDNEY.	TRINCOMALEE, CAPETOWN, TRINIDAD, NEW YORK.	NEW YORK, CLYDE.
SYDNEY, FREMANTLE, CAPETOWN, SIMONSTOWN, FREETOWN, CLYDE.	SYDNEY, FREMANTLE, TRINCOMALEE, SUEZ, TRINCOMALEE, FREMANTLE, SYDNEY.	NEW YORK, BOSTON, KEY WEST, RIO DE JANEIRO, CAPETOWN, FREMANTLE, SYDNEY.	CLYDE, NEW YORK, CLYDE, (2 voyages).
CLYDE, FREETOWN, CAPETOWN, SIMONSTOWN, TRINCOMALEE, SINGAPORE, SYDNEY.	SYDNEY, HOBART, SYDNEY, FREMANTLE, TRINCOMALEE, SUEZ, TRINCOMALEE, FREMANTLE, SYDNEY, (2 voyages).	SYDNEY, FREMANTLE, CAPETOWN, RIO DE JANEIRO, NEW YORK.	CLYDE, BOSTON, NEW YORK, CLYDE.
SYDNEY, FREMANTLE, BOMBAY, FREMANTLE, SYDNEY.		NEW YORK, CLYDE.	CLYDE, FREETOWN, CAPETOWN, ADEN, SUEZ, MASSAWA, H.M. BASE EAST INDIES, FREMANTLE, SYDNEY, FREMANTLE, CAPETOWN, FREETOWN, CLYDE.
SYDNEY, FREMANTLE, TRINCOMALEE, FREMANTLE, SYDNEY.	SYDNEY, HOBART, SYDNEY, FREMANTLE, TRINCOMALEE, SUEZ, TRINCOMALEE.	CLYDE, FREETOWN, SIMONSTOWN, SUEZ, SIMONSTOWN, RIO DE JANEIRO, NEW YORK.	CLYDE, NEW YORK OR HALIFAX, CLYDE, (28 voyages).

NEWS IN [...]

[...]n New Guinea[...] [...]e now broken[...] [...]anese resistance[...] [...]he first French c[...] [...]ritish port since[...] [...]nce has now arr[...] [...]urst. It had[...] [...]ar, which is n[...] Allies.

[...]A. F. fighters [...] [...]s over North[...] [...]rday, without los[...] [...]er of enemy planes were [...]d, but these did not attempt [...]position.

Imagination.

Believe only what you read in the *Ocean Daily News*, and remember—Rumour Lies!

[...] overheated "up-top" and "down-below."

You would be wrong if you spoke of the "sharp" or the "blunt" end. They are known as the bows or the stern.

[...]downstairs, but [...] When the operation has just begun, we are "weighing the anchor." As soon as it is clear of the water, but not secured, then it is "aweigh." Not until it is secured for sea is it said to be "weighed."

85

Loaded with 10,000 to 15,000 passengers, the conditions aboard the Queen Mary were extremely crowded. To accommodate the extraordinary number of men, each standee berth had two or three occupants, sleeping in shifts. The berths were stacked up to six high with only eighteen inches of space between them. To turn over in the middle of the night, one had to get out of bed. Yet, with 15,000 aboard, enough berths were not available, even with the men sleeping in shifts. Thousands of soldiers had to bed down on the ship's upper decks. A rotation system was implemented whereby a man would sleep one night on deck and the next night in a berth. Many men preferred sleeping on the upper decks because they felt they would be safer if the Queen Mary were torpedoed.

The system devised by the British crew and American military commanders of the Queen Mary to achieve the highest efficiency and comfort on the over-crowded ship was ingenious. The *Queen* was divided into red, white, and blue zones, with each man issued a button in one of the three colors. He was restricted to that zone of the ship. The system made it possible to load the *Queen* in New York and unload in Gourock in amazingly short periods of time.

The troops were served two meals a day, breakfast and dinner. At each meal, the men took extra servings of fruit and snacks to eat during the long period between meals. Still, the amount of food needed for each voyage was staggering. During the five-day crossing, the men consumed 155,000 pounds of meat and poultry; 21,500 pounds of bacon and ham; 124,000 pounds of potatoes; 76,000 pounds of flour and cereals; 53,000 pounds of butter, eggs, and powdered milk; 31,000 pounds of coffee, tea, and sugar; 31,000 pounds of canned fruit; 18,000 pounds of jams and jellies; 4,600 pounds of cheese; 400 pounds of candy; 5,000 cartons of cigarettes; and 40,000 bottles of soft drinks.

Meal preparation for passengers and crew put a dreadful strain on the ship's catering department. Cooks worked around the clock in shifts — as breakfast was being served, a host of cooks and assistants were preparing the next meal.

During her wartime service, the Queen Mary hosted Prime Minister Winston Churchill on a number of occasions when he visited the United States to attend war conferences. Churchill always traveled under the pseudonym Colonel Warden, a code name used to confuse enemy agents interested in the *Queen's* passenger list. In May 1943, August 1943, and September 1944, Churchill sailed aboard the *Queen* to the Trident, Quadrant, and Octagon war conferences, the top-secret meetings with top-level American and other Allied war leaders. While aboard the Queen Mary in August 1943, Churchill first reviewed the plans for the D-Day invasion and affixed his signature.

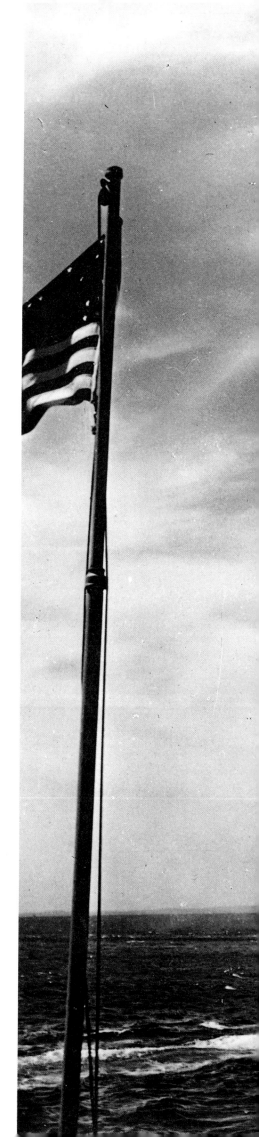

Opposite Page:
Escort ships and anti-submarine blimp greet the Queen Mary *as she nears New York Harbor.*

So effective was she as a troopship, Adolf Hitler put a bounty on the Queen Mary. He promised Germany's highest military honor, the Knight's Cross of the Iron Cross with Oak Leaves, to anyone who could sink her. As an added incentive, he also offered a cash reward of $250,000. But the liner used her great speed to avoid contact with enemy vessels. Several U-boat commanders later swore they had spotted the Queen Mary through their periscopes, only to have her quickly steam out of range. She was hunted, but never snared.

The Queen Mary's wartime job was not finished at the war's end, as she shouldered the Herculean task of returning war-weary American and Canadian soldiers to their homelands and families. The wounded were first, with the *Queen* fitted out as a floating hospital including surgical and intensive care units in the larger lounges and drawing rooms. Then the troops. Voyage after voyage, the Queen Mary carried the triumphant soldiers home to their wives and children after months of arduous warfare.

Following the return of the soldiers, the Queen Mary was conscripted into further service as another type of transport. Thousands of American and Canadian soldiers married Europeans during the war, and the brides were anxious to join their husbands. On thirteen voyages, the *Queen* safely transported 22,000 war brides and children to their husbands in the United States and Canada. The ship's lounges and drawing rooms resembled giant nurseries, with diapers and baby clothes drying on makeshift clotheslines. Four new American and Canadian citizens were born on these trips.

Home from the war. The Queen *receives a joyous welcome in Southampton, her home port, as she returns for the first time after nearly six years of wartime service.*

Opposite Page:
The war's over! Triumphant and excited members of the 30th Infantry Division unfurl their banner as the Queen *departs Southampton. The exuberant soldiers are anxious to get "Stateside."*

89

*"**GI** brides" with children aboard the* Queen *enroute to New York, March 1946.*

On September 27, 1946, the Queen Mary docked at Southampton from Halifax, Nova Scotia, concluding her last voyage as a troop carrier. She was finally demobilized.

During her war service, the *Queen* carried more than 800,000 servicemen, traveled more than 600,000 miles, and played a part in every major Allied campaign of World War II. She served as Winston Churchill's seaborne headquarters; carried American, Canadian, and Australian troops; transported German and Italian POWs; and served as a hospital ship and bridal transport — all without sighting or being attacked by an enemy vessel or aircraft. With all her protective armament, the Queen Mary never fired a gun in anger.

A GI bride and her children take a turn around Sun Deck, March 1946. The Queen *carried more than 22,000 women and children to the United States and Canada, where they rejoined husbands and fathers.*

Bathed and powdered, a happy baby stares curiously at the photographer. The woman on the bunk puts on a little powder of her own.

Together, the *Mary* and the *Elizabeth* had been the equal of a fleet of twenty lesser ships. Sir Winston Churchill, in his memoirs, conceded that the Queen Mary had been instrumental in shortening the war. Cunard Chairman Sir Percy Bates commented, " . . . I would like to think the two ships shortened the war by one year." The Queen Mary, pride of Great Britain, had endeared herself to millions of American soldiers, and, indeed, the entire free world owed her a great debt of gratitude.

If the Queen Mary had been built just for wartime use, she would have justified her construction costs. But the *Queen* still had a glorious future ahead of her.

The Statue of Liberty welcomes a shipload of new citizens to the United States. The brides, married to American soldiers, soon will be reunited with their husbands.

After many months of reconversion, she was ready to resume her place as *Queen of the Atlantic.* To restore the passenger liner to her former glory was a gargantuan task. Furniture, artwork, and other fittings were gathered from warehouses around the world and shipped to Southampton. All evidence of the years of difficult military use had to be erased from the *Queen's* lounges and cabins. Bit by bit, workmen gradually reclaimed the look of elegance and sophistication with which the *Queen* had been designed and constructed.

Finally, the Queen Mary was ready to begin again the job for which she was created. For the next twenty years, the Queen Mary and her sistership would be a moving bridge across the Atlantic, safely transporting millions of passengers between two continents now at peace.

Opposite Page:
The Queen Mary *steams gracefully past downtown Manhattan with a full load of happy homeward-bound soldiers.*

Opposite Page:
As the Queen *approaches her Pier 90 berth in New York, returning troops receive a warm and well-deserved welcome.*

RETURN TO
PEACETIME SERVICE:

THE QUEEN MARY LEGACY

*Winston Churchill, seated in the First Class Drawing Room, returns
on the* Queen Mary *from talks with President Harry Truman in 1951.*

Chapter IV

On July 31, 1947, the RMS Queen Mary sailed from Southampton on her first peacetime voyage in nearly eight years, performing the task for which she had been built: the weekly two-ship express service to New York. The two great *Queens of the Atlantic* ran like clockwork — week after week, month after month — providing regular mail and passenger service. As the *Mary* sailed from Southampton, the *Elizabeth* departed from New York, passing each other in mid-Atlantic. In calm, clear water, the sisterships' Captains charted their courses to within a few thousand feet of each other. No matter what the time when the two ships passed, night or day, hundreds of enthusiastic passengers lined the rails, waving and cheering as the two superliners swept past one another at a combined speed of more than 60 miles per hour.

On almost every voyage, the Queen Mary carried notable passengers: a foreign dignitary, a film star, a literary great. Great Britain's Prime Minister, Sir Winston Churchill, and his wife were aboard for the westbound crossing in January 1953, enroute to Washington DC for a series of conferences with President-Elect Dwight D Eisenhower And in November 1954, Elizabeth, the Queen Mother, returned to England aboard the Queen Mary, ending a goodwill tour of America. During the voyage, the Queen Mother continued to spread good will as she visited the various crew and working areas of the ship, greeting and chatting with members of the crew.

Workmen use their brushes as paddles in the drydock at Southampton in December 1954. The Queen *is receiving her annual overhaul, and the men will wash down the liner's hull as the water recedes.*

*The work crews prepare the liner to
return to transatlantic passenger service
in 1947. Here, the librarian inventories
books in the Second Class Library while
workmen reinstall fixtures.*

The weekly transatlantic crossings didn't always run like clockwork. As the Queen Mary approached New York Harbor on February 6, 1953, Captain Donald Sorrell received the news that all of New York's tugboats were out of service due to a workers' strike. Cunard officials, hoping to maintain the *Queen*'s tight schedule, radioed Sorrell, asking if he could dock the Queen Mary without tugboats. Although only his second voyage as Relief Captain, 5'4" Sorrell, a man with enormous confidence in his ship and his own skill, radioed back, "Certainly! I will be delighted."

It was a Herculean task. Normally, four or five tugboats were required to dock the Queen Mary in New York. Her four massive thirty-five-ton propellers were intended to power the *Queen* at high speeds on the open sea — they were not designed to maneuver the giant liner in close quarters, where scant inches meant the difference between success and disaster.

The docking process was further complicated by the slow-moving but powerful current of the Hudson River. But, undaunted, Captain Sorrell carefully maneuvered the *Queen* up the Hudson to Pier 90. Proceeding to the bridge wing, he carried with him a special sighting instrument — a crude block of wood sporting a formation of nails — he had invented for just such an emergency. He lined up the *Queen* to her dock with the instrument, then slowly inched the great ship forward, cautioning the Quartermaster to hold her straight and steady. A tiny lifeboat was dispatched from the nearby Cunarder Caronia to carry the docking lines to the pier.

As the *Queen*'s bow moved past the end of the pier, it seemed Sorrell had achieved the impossible on his first attempt. But suddenly, the current of the Hudson River caught the ship's stern, edging it menacingly toward the pier. The massive bow, which had cut a light cruiser in half during World War II, swung toward the West Side Highway. At even the slowest speed, the *Queen*'s weight and momentum could greatly damage the pier. Spectators crowding the dock hurriedly moved back, expecting the worst.

On the bridge, Captain Sorrell recognized the danger and calmly ordered the Quartermaster "All astern." Just in time, the ship moved back from the dock to mid-channel. Sorrell decided to try again. Using the strong Hudson River current to his advantage, he moved the *Queen* forward into the dock. Using the ship's lines and docking equipment, he brought the Queen Mary into the dock on his second attempt, calmly telling the Quartermaster, "All stop. Finished with engines." The next day, Captain Sorrell's achievement was proclaimed in headlines around the world.

*During the ship's 1951 overhaul in Southampton, workmen rehang the
First Class Main Lounge curtains after cleaning.*

Screen star Marlene Dietrich clutches her hat on the breezy Sports Deck as the Queen Mary *travels at more than 30 miles per hour.*

Only one other captain had previously docked the Queen Mary without the aid of tugboats. In October 1938, Commodore R. B. Irving also accomplished this amazing feat in the remarkable time of thirty-four minutes, the same docking time needed with the aid of twelve tugboats.

The post-war 1940s and the decade of the 1950s proved to be a time of prosperity for the Queen Mary and the Queen Elizabeth. Month after month, they continued the weekly transatlantic schedule, carrying full complements of contented passengers.

But with the advent of jet aircraft and improved air safety records in the 1960s, the liners' future became cloudy. While the sisterships took nearly five days, jets crossed the Atlantic in seven hours. In the new era of the jet age, speed became king, and the *Queen's* passenger loads began to dwindle. By the mid-sixties, the Queen Mary carried just a fraction of her former passenger complements.

Fred Astaire pauses at a stairway for ship's photographer.

Douglas Fairbanks, Jr. and Norma Shearer dance.

February 13, 1952. The Duke of Windsor, formerly King Edward VIII, in the First Class Drawing Room during a press conference.

David Niven breaks into a lively Scottish Fling upon arrival at Southampton in July 1947. He was on his way to star the London Film production of "Bonnie Prince Charlie."

Clark Gable with ship's Chief Steward.

Handsome and jauntily attired Victor Mature braves a cool breeze on the liner's Sun Deck.

Glamorous Gloria Swanson strikes an alluring pose during a transatlantic crossing.

Olympic swimmer and gold medalist Johnny Weissmuller watches the horizon from Sports Deck.

Bob Hope gives actress Loretta Young one of his trademark leers upon arrival at Southampton in November 1947. Fellow travelers are actors Robert Montgomery, Loretta Young, and her husband, Craig Stevens.

In an attempt to increase the *Queen*'s revenue, Cunard reduced the frequency of Atlantic crossings and used her for a number of short cruises to various ports. The Queen Mary was unsuccessful as a cruise ship, however. She was too large to dock at most harbors, requiring her passengers to go ashore via small launches. Finally, in May 1967, after several years of multi-million-dollar losses, Cunard announced that both the *Queen*'s would be sold.

Numerous proposals were put forth for the Queen Mary, ranging from the practical to the bizarre. Several cities, including New York, wanted to use the ship as a youth hostel or floating classroom facility. An imaginative Texan suggested welding together the *Mary* and the *Elizabeth* to make the world's largest catamaran. But in a sealed-bid auction, the City of Long Beach, California, became the new owners of the Queen Mary with a bid of $3.45 million and plans to convert the ship into a floating hotel, tourist attraction, and maritime museum.

Cunard officials then met with the Long Beach delegation to discuss transporting the *Queen* from England to California. Cunard proposed sailing the Queen Mary to Long Beach with a skeleton crew, but Long Beach officials insisted on bringing the ship home in grand style with a full complement of passengers. In fact, one of the stipulations of the bid was that the Queen Mary be booked for one last cruise from Southampton to Long Beach. Cunard tried to dissuade the delegation from booking a passenger cruise, but they were adamant. Reluctantly, Cunard agreed to help with the planning of the voyage.

The problems involved were tremendous. Too large to pass through the Panama Canal, the Queen Mary would have to sail around Cape Horn on the southernmost tip of South America. The ship would cross the equator

Seductive oriental beauty Anna May Wong relaxes in ship's First Class Main Lounge in 1937.

Approximately five hours out of New York on July 17, 1957, the Queen Mary *answered a distress call from the USS* Somersworth. *Four injured sailors were transferred by lifeboat to the* Queen's *hospital for immediate treatment after which they were put aboard the USS* Sunbird *to be transported to a shoreside hospital.*

RESCUE AT SEA

The Queen Mary had many adventures during her thirty-one years at sea, but none were more exciting than a daring mid-Atlantic rescue on January 29, 1955. As the Queen wallowed heavily in high seas whipped by gale-force winds, stewards served a sparsely-attended afternoon tea in the main dining room. In the radioroom, meanwhile, the operator jotted down an urgent request for help: "TWO SEAMEN FALLEN FROM TWIN DECK TO HOLD #2 STOP THEY MORTALLY WOUNDED STOP PLEASE ANY SHIP WITH DOCTOR."

Three hundred and twenty-three miles from the Queen Mary, aboard the 7,100-ton Panamanian freighter Liberator, two injured men were dying from a lack of medical assistance.

Within minutes, the Liberator's message was delivered to Captain Donald Sorrell on the bridge of the Queen Mary. Captain Sorrell, quickly considered the situation. Other ships were closer to the Liberator, but the Queen had two surgeons and a hospital with medical equipment. Weighing two men's lives against the economics of deviating from the ship's tight schedule, he made his decision at once. At full speed, the Queen Mary turned and raced toward the Liberator.

The Queen reached the Liberator at 1:30 a.m. the following morning. With moderate-gale winds beating the sea into froth, Captain Sorrell switched on his searchlights and delicately maneuvered the massive ship into position between the smaller vessel and the screaming winds.

Senior First Officer Leslie Goodier mustered his crew and boarded the lifeboat on Sun Deck, lowering the small craft eighty-five feet into the sea. The wind billowed against the large surface of the Queen's side, causing her to roll heavily and making the lowering a dangerous operation. Huddled in the boat was the ship's junior surgeon, Dr. Timothy Yates, who volunteered to board the Liberator

and attend the injured seamen.

Tossed to and fro by the towering waves, the boat took eleven minutes to cross to the freighter. As the small craft slammed against the Liberator's hull, Dr. Yates leaped from the boat to cling precariously to a rope boarding ladder before being hauled aboard by the freighter's crewmen.

The lifeboat could not remain alongside in the furious seas. The craft was in danger of capsizing, and the crew was suffering from exposure. Goodier was forced to return to the Queen Mary, and the lifeboat was hoisted aboard the liner.

Goodier, reporting to the Captain, stated, "It will be absolutely impossible to get the men off in these conditions." Acting on the Senior First Officer's report, the Captain radioed the Liberator, "DOCTOR YATES. ARE YOU PREPARED TO STAY ABOARD?" The doctor's reply came quickly. "NO, THIS SHIP GOING TO CANADA! WE ARE READY TO LOWER PATIENTS NOW IF YOU ARE READY."

Sorrell murmured to the bridge crew, "He doesn't realize how bad it is. We'll have to send a message telling him he must stay." They all knew the injured men's chances of survival were poor if they could not be transferred to the Queen's hospital.

A quiet voice broke the joyless reflection. "I think I can do it, sir, if you will let me get another volunteer crew," said the Queen's Chief Officer, Lt. Commander Phillips A. Read. "You're quite sure," asked the Captain. "Certain," Read replied.

Read's plan required perfect timing. The Captain would bring the Queen Mary as close as possible to the Liberator, holding the liner broadside to the shrieking wind to give the boat crew a brief lull in which to lower the wounded men into the lifeboat. It was a risky procedure. A large ship stopped in the water is difficult to maneuver. Because

the exposed area of her hull and superstructure is three times her underwater area, a ship exposed to high winds could move sideways, accelerating rapidly in just minutes.

Read and his crew lowered their boat and roller-coastered through twenty-five-foot waves to the side of the Liberator. With his boat in position, Read used a signal lamp to alert the Queen's captain. Acting quickly, Sorrell eased the Queen Mary alongside the freighter. The plan worked–the Liberator lay in the calm of the lee provided by the massive ocean liner.

Within minutes, Dr. Yates and the two seamen were lowered into the lifeboat. But the Queen Mary was drifting dangerously close to the Liberator, threatening to crush the much smaller vessel. The instant the lifeboat cleared the freighter's side, Captain Sorrell ordered the Mary's engines full astern. The four giant screws foamed the sea as the ship knifed backward, away from the wallowing freighter, the Queen's bow clearing the Liberator by only fifty feet!

As the lifeboat was hauled up the side of the Queen Mary, it swung inboard, smashing hard against the liner's steel hull. Read, unprepared for the impact, was hurled overboard into the churning sea. Reacting instantly, an AB (Able-Bodied Seaman) grabbed Read's feet, yanking him back into the boat just as it lifted clear of the sea's surface.

The unconscious seamen, carried to the Queen Mary's hospital where the ship's doctors attended them, later recovered fully in a Southampton hospital.

Perhaps more than any single incident in the Queen Mary's illustrious career, this daring sea rescue illustrated that, beneath the glamour and elegance, her captain and crew were brilliant seamen, with the courage and stamina to challenge the fury of the North Atlantic.

Opposite Page:
First Class Swimming Pool. The Queen Mary *offered two swimming pools, both indoors because of the often inclement weather. This two-level pool was the most elegant, boasting handmade tile and a simulated mother-of-pearl ceiling.*

The First Class Dining Room is decorated with beautiful paintings, wood carvings, and glasswork. This painting by Dame Laura Knight, entitled The Mills Circus, *is from one of the private dining rooms adjoining the main hall.*

twice, steaming into hot tropical climates for which she was not equipped, having air-conditioning only in one second-class and six first-class public rooms. Fuel and water difficulties were also staggering. A route had to be devised that included refueling ports large enough to accommodate her 1,019½-foot length and 40-foot-deep draught, and close enough together to replenish her fresh-water supply before it was completely exhausted.

Eventually, the problems were solved, and the Queen Mary was ready to begin the thirty-nine-day voyage billed as her "Last Great Cruise."

Departing from Southampton, England, on October 31, 1967, the Queen Mary attracted worldwide attention as she commenced her last crossing, a voyage that would add many new records to her already distinguished career. Thousands of Britons turned out to wish their beloved *Queen* a tearful farewell. As the ship eased away from the dock, the Queen Mary's 310-foot-long paying-off pennant streamed from her mainmast, each year of service represented by ten feet of colorful banner.

The First Class Main Lounge on Promenade Deck. The beautiful mural over the fireplace titled Unicorns in Battle *was created by Alfred Oakley and Gilbert Bayes. It is a Gesso panel – a wood carving overlayed with plaster, then decorated with gold and silver gilt.*

THE QUEEN MARY CREW

The number of crew personnel varied from voyage to voyage depending upon the number of passengers. However, although the number of catering staff and stewards fluctuated, the deck department usually remained constant.

Captain: 1.
Staff Captain: 1.
Deck Department: 116 total.

Navigating Officers: 8–Chief, Senior First, Junior First, Senior Second, Junior Second, Senior Third, Intermediate Third, Junior Third.
Radio Officers: 12.
Carpenter: 1.
Assistant Carpenters: 4.
Bosun: 1.
Bosun's Mates: 3.
Master at Arms (MAA): 8.
Fire Patrol: 6.
Storekeeper: 1.
Lamp Trimmer: 1.
Quartermasters: 6.
Able-Bodied Seamen: 57.
Ordinary Seamen and Boy Seamen: 8.

Pursers: 58 total.
Purser: 1.
Staff Purser: 1.
Assistant Pursers: 16.
Assistant Pursers, Women: 4.
Baggage Masters: 3.
Interpreter: 1.
Printers: 5.

Musicians: 20.
Photographers: 3.
Telephone Operators: 4.

Medical Staff: 14 total.
Surgeons: 2.
Nursing Sisters: 4.
Physiotherapist: 1.
Dispenser: 1.
Hospital Attendants: 3.
Officers' Stewards: 3.

Engine Department: 254 total.

Engineering Officers: 64.
Electrical Engineering Officers: 22.
Sanitary Engineer: 1.
Boiler Maker: 1.
Plumbers: 6.
Engineering Writers: 2.
Leading Hands: 3.
Storekeeper: 1.
Assistant Storekeepers: 3.
Refrigeration Attendant: 1.
Electric Greasers: 6.
Deck and Main Greasers: 45.
Firemen: 42.
Trimmers: 46.
Trimmers' Peggys: 8.
Cinema Operators: 3.

Catering Department: 829 total.

Chief Steward: 1.
Second Steward: 1.
Restaurant Managers: 2.
Bedroom Stewards: 181.

Waiters and Commissary Waiters (Trainees): 204.
Night Stewards and Assistants: 36.
Officers' Stewards: 32.
Deck and Public Room Stewards: 39.
Kitchen Staff: 158.

Female Staff: 73 total.
Stewardesses: 44.
Nursery Stewardesses: 3.
Bath Attendants: 10.
Shop Assistants: 7.
Swimming Pool Attendants: 2.
Hairdressers: 6.
Turkish Bath Attendant: 1.

Other Personnel: 102.
Pantrymen, Bellboys, Shoeboys, Linen Storekeepers, Chief Storekeeper and Assistants, Clothes Pressers, Utilitymen, Gardeners, Writers, Lift (Elevator) Attendants, Barbers, Physical Training Instructors, Swimming Pool Attendants, Masseurs, and Turkish Bath Attendants.

Summary: 1,273 total.

Captain: 1. .
Staff Captain: 1.
Deck Department: 188.
Engine Department: 254.
Catering Department: 829.

The per-day cost of operating the ship was: 1936–$30,000.

1956–$56,000.   1967–$70,000.

The Royal Marine Corps band played "Auld Lang Syne" as Royal Navy helicopters flew overhead in a giant anchor formation. Hundreds of boats and ships of all sizes swarmed about the harbor as the *Queen* prepared to sail, filling the air with the sounds of horns and whistles.

This Last Great Cruise was the *Queen*'s longest peacetime voyage, 14,559 miles, and took her to some of the world's most exotic ports: Lisbon, Portugal; Las Palmas, Canary Islands; Rio de Janeiro, Brazil; Valparaiso, Chile; Callao, Peru; Balboa, Panama; and Acapulco, Mexico.

To save fuel, only two of the ship's four engines and propellers were to be used during the voyage. But, with the rough weather and the enormous drag of the two unused propellers, it soon became apparent that the *Queen* would have trouble maintaining the planned schedule. Her first stop at Lisbon was, in fact, delayed when the giant liner missed the high tide necessary for her safe entry into the harbor.

During the first long leg of the voyage, the 3,500-mile expanse between Las Palmas and Rio de Janeiro, some passengers complained of the heat as the ship passed through tropical waters. Most, however, remained cheerful, having been warned about the heat before booking passage.

An alert crew constantly mans the wheelhouse, command center of the huge liner.

Starting platform in the after engine room. A portion of two massive turbines are visible in the lower part of the photograph.

Whenever weather permitted, the captains of the two Queens steered their ships to pass as close as possible in mid-Atlantic. As the two ships steamed towards each other at combined speeds of more than 60 miles per hour, the captains would salute each other's ship with three long blasts of their whistles.

Hundreds of boats and thousands of spectators bid the Queen a fond farewell as the liner departs New York for the last time on September 22, 1967.

Opposite Page:
Cunard publicity posters offer a chance to sail on the Queen Mary's final cruises.

Be one of the last to sail on the Queen Mary. (unrepeatable offer!) **Choose from these historic farewell sailings.**

6 farewell transatlantic crossings.

Join in the fun as the Queen Mary crosses the Atlantic for the last few times. 12 day all-inclusive round trips, taking in a night's stop in New York. Fares start at £171.10.0.

Departure dates from Southampton.

July 6th, July 20th (Nightlife Special), August 2nd, August 16th, August 30th, September 16th.

2 farewell cruises.

The very last Cunard sailings of the Queen Mary. For 7 days, live it up like never before, as you sail to the Canaries on the voyage of a lifetime. Fares start at £70.

Queen Mary autumn cruise to Las Palmas and Gibraltar. Leaves Southampton Friday 29th September. 7 days cruise from £70.

Queen Mary final cruise to Las Palmas. Leaves Southampton Friday 13th October. 6 days cruise from £70.

Hurry-or you'll miss the boat! Ask inside for details.

CUNARD
WHITE STAR

R.M.S "QUEEN
MARY"

QUEEN MARY

As the Queen Mary *leaves Southampton on her final voyage October 31, 1967, Royal Navy helicopters fly overhead in the formation of a giant anchor.*

Captain and crewmen pose on the Promenade Deck with the Queen Mary's *310-foot "paying off" pennant, a traditional streamer flown on a ship's last voyage. (Ten feet represents each year of service, hence the* Queen Mary's *pennant was 310 feet for her 31 years of service.) Pictured from left to right are F. H. Egerton, Boatswain; John Treasure Jones; The* Queen Mary's *last captain, J. S. Allen, Chief Deck Steward; and R. Wilson, Quartermaster.*

End of an era! Passengers party for the last time on December 8, 1967, in the Queen Mary's elegant First Class Main Lounge.

After a stopover in Rio de Janeiro, the *Queen* prepared to round Cape Horn. Crewmen tied down everything moveable in anticipation of the Horn's notorious rough seas and violent storms, neither of which materialized. Hundreds of passengers lined the decks, standing in the cold rain, to witness the historic moment when the Queen Mary rounded the Cape. She was the largest ship to carry the greatest number of passengers ever around Cape Horn.

Many passengers were not content to just sail around Cape Horn. Some rode around the Horn in English double-decker buses parked on the Main Deck, where two of the bright red buses were lashed, on their way to Long Beach. Dr. Orville W. Cole, Long Beach physician and past president of the Long Beach Chamber of Commerce, sold tickets to "Ride Around the Cape" as a fundraiser. The idea was a sellout, and the money

RADIOGRAM
CUNARD STEAM-SHIP CO. LTD.
RADIO SERVICES OPERATED BY
INTERNATIONAL MARINE RADIO CO., LTD.

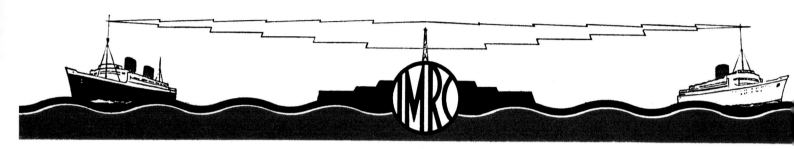

Received by R.M.S. "QUEEN MARY"   Date......24/9/67.....................   Form B.52M
Printed in En

PREAMBLE:	PREFIX	OFFICE OF ORIGIN NUMBER	NO. OF WORDS	DATE	TIME	SERVICE INSTRUCTIONS		
RADIO:	MSG	QUEEN ELIZABETH	N/C	24				

TO	CAPTAIN TREASURE JONES			
			RECEIVED	
	QUEEN MARY	FROM	TIME	B
		GBSS	1452Z	JW

YOU can telephone or telegraph to any part of the world from this ship. You can thus use the radio service to reply to this message, to reserve accommodation on shore, and make railway and aeroplane reservations from mid-ocean in advance of your arrival.

You can also communicate with your home or business at any time during the voyage.

Enquiries respecting this message should be made at the International Marine Radio Co. Ltd's Radio Office on board, or addressed to the International Marine Radio Co. Ltd., Peall Road, Croydon, Surrey, and must be accompanied by this form.

Please read on the back of this form the conditions under which this message has been transmitted.

COMMEMORATING VESSEL'S LAST VOYAGE

(signature) CHIEF RADIO OFFI

1400Z POS 4938N 3005W CO 259 SPEED 27.5 KTS WIND NW 6 BARO 996 CLOUDY AND CLEAR WE HAD A BIT OF A BLOW YESTERDAY JUST OFF IRELAND BUT IT LOOKS AS IF THOUGH YOU SHOULD HAVE FOLLOWING WINDS . IT IS A SAD MOMENT AS THESE TWO GREAT SHIPS PASS FOR THE LAST TIME BUT WE HOPE TO SEE YOU SHORTLY AFTER MIDNIGHT NEW TIME AND MOST OF MY PASSENGERS ARE WAITING UP FOR THIS HISTORIC EVENT HOPE THAT YOU AND YOUR WIFE ENJOY THE TRIP ROUND CAPE HORN REGARDS AND BEST WISHES

GEOFFREY

GEORGE V *PARIS*   SAVOY *London*   WALDORF-ASTORIA *N YC*

Shortly before the two great Queens met for the last time at sea, Commodore Geoffrey Marr of the Queen Elizabeth sent this radiogram to Captain John Treasure Jones of the Queen Mary. As the message indicates, the sisterships passed each other in the darkness after midnight on September 25, 1967.

...aming up the California coastline, the Queen Mary *is greeted by an aerial "...lcome wagon" as a Douglas DC-9 flies over the ship and drops carnations on ...upper decks. When the* Queen *approached New York Harbor at the end of her ...iden voyage on June 1, 1936, Eddie Rickenbacker welcomed the ship in the ...ie manner from a DC-2.*

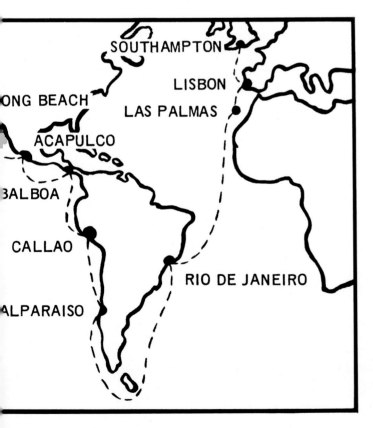

Map shows the route of the Queen's 14,000-mile voyage from Southampton to Long Beach.

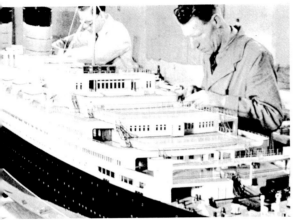

Craftsmen at work on one of Cunard's models of the Queen Mary *in 1935. The model is 1/49th the actual size of the* Queen, *constructed on a scale of 1/4"=1 foot, is 21 feet long, and weighs more than one ton. The model was constructed from a single log of 200-year-old white mahogany from Africa. The log was first cut into planks, then laminated together for greater strength to prevent warping or cracking. The model has more than 4,600 individual fittings on it. Now displayed aboard the* Queen Mary *in Long Beach, California, it is on loan from the South Street Seaport Museum in New York.*

was donated to a school in Valparaiso, Long Beach's sister city and the *Queen's* next port.

Another enterprising passenger, Dutch Miller of Long Beach, captain of the city's lifeguards, was in the first-class pool swimming laps as the ship rounded the Cape. He now claims to be the only man ever to swim around Cape Horn.

At Valparaiso, Long Beach Mayor Edwin Wade boarded the *Queen* for the final days of the voyage, and at Acapulco, dozens of dignitaries and news reporters embarked for the jaunt to Long Beach, the final cruise of the Queen Mary's career. Passengers were filled with mixed emotions: sadness that the great liner was ending her career, and happiness that they were able to be a part of the Last Great Cruise. In fact, hundreds of passengers, including Dr. Cole, banded together to form the Queen Mary Club, an official committee of the Long Beach Chamber of Commerce. Dedicated to perpetuate the historic achievements and traditions of the *Queen*, the club is still active with a membership of more than 500.

Five hundred miles from Long Beach, the *Queen* received a special welcoming tribute. A Douglas Aircraft DC-9 jetliner flew low over the Queen Mary, dropping thousands of carnations onto her upper decks, a re-creation of the June 1, 1936, event at which Eddie Rickenbacker showered her with flowers from his DC-2 as she entered New York Harbor on her maiden voyage.

At Long Beach, the immensely popular *Queen* was greeted by a flotilla of more than 5,000 vessels including rowboats, sailboats, luxury yachts, Coast Guard cutters, fire boats, and even the nuclear cruiser USS Long Beach, while thousands of spectators crowded the shoreline.

On her bridge, Captain John Treasure Jones watched apprehensively as the thousands of small crafts converged on the *Queen*, anticipating that so many vessels maneuvering in such a small space would undoubtedly incur a collision. Jones looked at the radar scope. Instead of the normal tiny blips, it showed a solid lighted mass, so densely packed were the vessels around the *Queen*.

Through the mass of vessels, tugboats eased the *Queen* to a Pier E berth in the Long Beach Harbor. There, at 12:07 p.m., Captain Jones sadly stepped up to the bridge telegraphs and signaled "finished with engines." The Queen Mary's thirty-one years of service at sea had come to an end.

The Last Great Cruise was a bittersweet voyage — the passengers realized that the cruise marked the end of a glorious era in steamship travel. The *Queen of the Atlantic* would retire in the Pacific, in a city she had never visited. But not for her the breaker's hammer. Long Beach was not an ending; it was the beginning of a brand-new career.

The emerging skyline of Long Beach, California, is the perfect backdrop for the Queen Mary. Permanently berthed on Pier J in the Port of Long Beach, the Queen of the Atlantic has been joined recently by Howard Hughes' famous seaplane, the Spruce Goose.

QUEEN·MARY·

Jack and Bonita Granville Wrather were frequent travelers on the Queen Mary. In 1980, Jack Wrather's company, the Wrather Corporation, assumed management of the ship's operations and added the Spruce Goose as an attraction in Long Beach.

Captain John W. Gregory, current master of the Queen Mary, carries on the finest traditions of the ship's maritime heritage. Captain Gregory is also an ordained minister and couples can now be married aboard the Queen Mary by the Captain, something that could never have happened during the ship's seagoing career.

VOYAGE 1002

At the 1934 launching of the Queen Mary, British psychic Mabel Fortescue-Harrison predicted, "Most of this generation will be gone, including myself, when this event occurs; however, the Queen Mary, launched today, will know its greatest fame and popularity when she never sails another mile and never carries another passenger."

Her prophecy is coming true today in Long Beach, California, where each day thousands of eager visitors flock to board history's most famous ocean liner. They walk awestruck through her elegant public rooms and marvel at the size and power of her engines.

VOYAGE 1002

The Queen Mary made 1,001 Atlantic crossings during her thirty-one years of passenger service, and carried the most glamourous, the most famous people in the world. Now you, too, can sail on the Queen Mary, back to her glorious heyday of transatlantic splendor. See where Winston Churchill took tea and where Fred Astaire danced. Walk the *Queen*'s decks and join in the excitement as you set sail on a voyage of discovery, a voyage of imagination. Book passage on the Queen Mary for Voyage 1002, your own personal journey into nostalgia.

THE HOTEL

As a guest of the Hotel Queen Mary, you will occupy one of the ship's original first-class staterooms. You can still have breakfast in bed, but the *Queen*, known for her excellent cuisine, now as well as then, also offers a choice of several outstanding on-board restaurants. Live music and dancing — so much a part of the Queen Mary's past — still fill her cocktail lounges and public rooms.

THE SHIPWALK

No visit to the ship would be complete without a tour. The self-guided Queen Mary Shipwalk combs the giant liner's bowels for a first-hand look at the one remaining massive engine room with its two 40,000 horsepower engines, and a stop at the special enclosure allowing an underwater view of one of the ship's huge thirty-five-ton propellers. Throughout the Shipwalk, special film, video, and pictorial presentations exhibit highlights of the *Queen*'s illustrious career. On the upper decks, stroll the promenade upon which the world's most distinguished figures walked, and step into the opulent beauty of the First-Class Main Lounge, with its three-story-high ceiling and lustrous wood paneling.

The ship's bridge and wheelhouse, whose gleaming brass speaks of an earlier age of steamship travel, is an adventure for everyone. Animated displays simulate the complexity of navigating the *Queen* across the trackless ocean, where unexpected perils test the abilities of the liner's crew.

Before disembarking the Queen Mary, visit the displays showing the differences between first-class staterooms and third-class cabins. For contrast, the troopship accommodations display demonstrates the crowded conditions endured by Allied soldiers during World War II crossings.

The Queen Mary, once the most famous ship to go to sea and now the most famous ship to come to see.